The Alpha Series

John Glenn

"In that day you shall know that I am in My Father, and you in Me, and I in you."
John 14:20

AuthorHouse™
1663 Liberty Drive, Suite 200
Bloomington, IN 47403
www.authorhouse.com
Phone: 1-800-839-8640

AuthorHouse™ UK Ltd.
500 Avebury Boulevard
Central Milton Keynes, MK9 2BE
www.authorhouse.co.uk
Phone: 08001974150

©2006 John Glenn. All rights reserved.

No part of this book may be reproduced, stored in a retrieval system, or transmitted by any means without the written permission of the author.

First published by AuthorHouse 10/25/2006

ISBN: 1-4259-5816-8 (sc)

LIbrary of Congress Control Number : 2006909552

Printed in the United States of America
Bloomington, Indiana

This book is printed on acid-free paper.

Alpha Series

DEDICATED TO:

My wife, Sandi, and my daughter, Angela,
for their willingness to live, daily,
the gospel this series proclaims.

Alpha Series

Preface

In October of 1988, within the regeneration ministries of *Faith Farm* in Ft. Lauderdale, Florida, I began to systematically teach the gospel of Jesus Christ to twelve men in a recovery program called "*Alpha*." Every six weeks I was challenged by a new class of men who were desperately searching for a way out of their dysfunctional life-styles. The only resource capable of successfully meeting that challenge was the gospel of Jesus Christ. This study guide and the companion video tapes record the practical application of the gospel of Jesus Christ to the life-controlling issues we all must face.

The *Alpha Series* falls naturally into three main parts. The first part (chapters 1-4) concerns the manner in which we all suffer from the effects of inherent sin within the human race. The objective in these chapters is to identify the underlying causes of our personal and relational problems.

The second part of the series (chapters 5-9), I refer to as the gospel for believers. By this, I mean the Gospel of Jesus Christ is far more than simply trusting Jesus so we do not have to go to hell when we die. It is the glorious message of being made new in Christ, that enables us to experience the abundant life that Jesus promised. It is by faith in who God has made us to be in Christ Jesus that we may truly experience hope concerning ourselves.

The last part of the series (chapter 9-12) describes the crowning glory of God's grace in allowing us to love others as Christ did. No recovery is ever complete until we are able to share God's love with those around us. Through our personal relationships with others we display the reality of the gospel in our daily lives.

It is my prayer that this study guide, along with the video tapes, will be a useful tool for the Body of Christ. It is being offered for the sole purpose of "equipping the saints for the work of the ministry." May our Lord Jesus Christ richly bless you and keep you in His grace.

John Glenn

Alpha Series

Acknowledgments:

To Jim and Karen Groth for the preparation of this manuscript.

To Bill Ellis and Don Johnson for your vision and willingness to start this project.

To all the brethren of the Family Worship Center in Indiantown, Florida, for your support in the initiation of this project.

To all the brethren of the Church in the Woods at Freedom Ranch, Okeechobee, Florida for your continuing support in this project.

To the many students of the Alpha Series who have received with gladness the gospel message and dedicated themselves to sharing it with others.

Alpha Series

TABLE OF CONTENTS

CHAPTER 1: BIBLICAL SELF-AWARENESS — 11
    WHO ARE YOU? — 11
    FAMILY IDENTITY — 17

CHAPTER 2: FOUNDATION OF OUR NEEDS — 25
    JESUS MEETS OUR PERSONAL NEEDS — 25
    OUR UNION WITH CHRIST — 33

CHAPTER 3: UNDERSTANDING OUR EMOTIONS — 39
    CATEGORIES OF EMOTION — 39
    EMOTIONAL HEALING — 47

CHAPTER 4: THE HEART OF THE PROBLEM — 57
    TRADITIONS OF MEN — 57
    HOW PROBLEMS DEVELOP — 65

CHAPTER 5: OUR TRUE IDENTITY — 73
    GOD'S REGENERATION PROGRAM — 73
    THE PROMISE OF VICTORY — 83

CHAPTER 6: THE MIRROR — 91
    THE OLD AND NEW COVENANTS — 91
    SLAVES TO RIGHTEOUSNESS — 97

CHAPTER 7: WHO SHALL DELIVER ME? — 103
    DEAD TO THE LAW — 103
    CONFLICT WITHOUT CONDEMNATION — 111

CHAPTER 8: SALVATION BY GRACE — 117
    THE FREEDOM OF THE SPIRIT — 117
    THE CALL TO FAITH — 125

CHAPTER 9: THE COMFORT OF THE SPIRIT — 131
    PERSONAL ASSURANCE OF THE SPIRIT — 131
    FACING TRIALS IN THE SPIRIT — 139

CHAPTER 10: ANOTHER COMFORTER ---------------------------------- 147
    RELATIONAL MINISTRY -- 147
    COMFORT IN RELATIONAL MINISTRY -------------------------------- 153

CHAPTER 11: ABIDING IN CHRIST ------------------------------------- 159
    THE VINE AND THE BRANCHES -- 159
    LIVING IN CHRIST'S LOVE --- 167

CHAPTER 12: THE OVERCOMER --------------------------------------- 173
    THE MINISTRY OF THE OVERCOMER --------------------------------- 173
    THE OVERCOMER'S CHURCH --- 179

APPENDIX: ALPHA STUDY GUIDE BIBLE REFERENCES -------------------- 187

BIBLICAL SELF-AWARENESS   Chapter 1
WHO ARE YOU?   Lesson 1

Who are you?
This is a simple but very profound question that we each *must* face *daily*. It's simple because it may be answered by supplying things like our name, our occupation, our race, our nationality, or some other general designation or label. However, it is very profound as well. The deeper we probe for an *accurate* answer the more we must learn about ourselves, and our own sense of identity. This can be difficult, but if we are to know the deepest and truest sense of our identity, it must be done.

> *"John Doe"*
> *"Salesman"*.
> *"American"*
> *"Son of..."*
> *"Wife of.."*
> *"Republican"*
> *"Methodist"*

If we press the question past the normal, simple and easy responses of name, occupation, and nationality, (i.e., "I'm John Doe," or "I'm a salesman," or "I'm an American,") we are forced to get a bit more personal. For instance, we may identify ourselves according to our relationships by saying, "I'm the son of George Doe," or "I'm the wife of John Doe,." We might also identify ourselves according to our political persuasion with, "I'm a Republican," or our religious preferences with "I'm a Methodist."

For those who are brave enough to honestly look at themselves, other identities, which are natural, begin to emerge. By breaking through the defense mechanisms of denial and projection, many will begin to identify themselves with such labels as *alcoholic, or addict, co-dependent, A.C.O.A. (Adult Child of an Alcoholic)*, or simply *dysfunctional*. Psychological testing may also result in a wide assortment of labels ranging from *personality disorders* to *psychotic states*.

> *"A.C.O.A*
> *"Alcoholic"*
> *"Addict"*
> *"Codependent"*

All of these and various other ways we identify ourselves by answering the question,

> *Personality disorders*
> *Psychotic states*

"Who are You?" are important in determining the quality of our lives. The psychology experts tell us repeatedly that our own self-image (who we think we are) is one of the most important factors that determines our emotional state, our behavior, and the quality of our relationships. The biblical proverb, "For as a man thinketh in his heart, so is he..." suggests that our self-image can actually become a self-fulfilling prophecy.

Personality theorist, Carl Rodgers, offers some insight to the importance of the way we identify ourselves. He noted that the way we see ourselves (self-image) may vary from the way others see us (other's image). Furthermore, the way others see us may also be

> *For as a man thinketh in his heart, so is he...*

Alpha Series
Biblical Self-Awareness

different from the way we really are (real-image). Rodgers suggested that the inner turmoil and conflict that leads to personal and relational dysfunction is a result of our self-image being different from that of others or who we really are (see figure 1).

The greater the difference between how we see ourselves, how others see us, and how we really are; the greater the inner turmoil and dysfunction in our lives. Likewise, the closer our own self-image lines up with who we really are, and ultimately, how others see us, the less inner conflict we experience and the healthier we become.

Biblical evidence to support Rodgers' explanation may be drawn from the Genesis record of the creation of man. This account provides us with a beginning point for defining who we really are. Once we have discovered our *real* image according to the absolute truth of the Word of God, we may then address the issues that concern lining up our own self-image with who God says we really are. As will be seen in later lessons, the process of lining up our own self-image with the real image that God has made us to be is the key to a healthier more functional life. As we discover the truth about who God has made us to be, we are set free to relate more honestly with others, and the inner turmoil is reduced.

Genesis 2:7

Then the LORD God formed man of dust from the ground, and breathed into his nostrils the breath of life; and man became a living being (nasb).

The main purpose of the Alpha Series is to answer the question "Who are You?" with biblical truth that provides a solid foundation for a healthier self-image. When we learn the gospel of good news about who God has made us to be, we can begin to experience the personal freedom and joy necessary to engage in healthier relationships with others. While we have all learned to identify ourselves according to our natural world view, these identities, whether they be positive or negative in nature, are essentially false because they either fail to consider, or outright deny, God's view of us. True identity, can only be derived from the Word of God which is by definition absolute truth. As a beginning step, to discover our true identity, let us consider how God made man.

Alpha Series
Biblical Self-Awareness

The Structure of Man

The record of Adam's creation in Genesis 2:7 reveals the marvelous way that God made man in his image. In this one verse is found all the components of man. The body is formed by God out of the *dust of the ground* which represents the various physical elements that constitute our physical nature. God breathed the *breath of life,* the spiritual component of man, into the body. Thus, man became a *living soul or personal being.*

> How were we made?
> What were we made of?
> What are the components of man?

The body, soul, and spirit of man are to be viewed as a very complex system of interactions between each of the components. The body comprises the physical nature, the soul reveals the personal nature, and the spirit constitutes the spiritual nature; all a constant dynamic interaction we call life. For the purposes of this series, we shall define these components of man as follows.

The Structural Components of Man

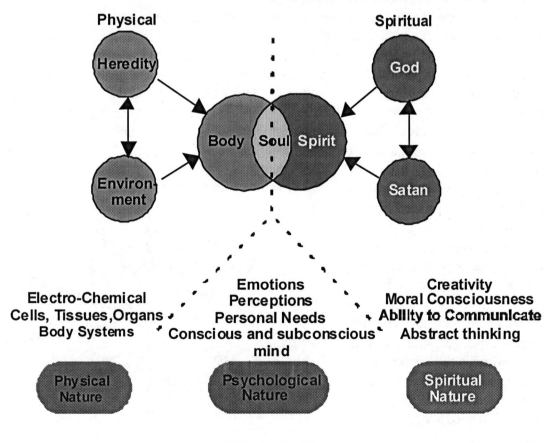

Who Are You?

Alpha Series
Biblical Self-Awareness

The body is that physical component of man which houses the spirit being. In his infinite wisdom and knowledge God fashioned the body of Adam to accomplish his purposes for humanity. While we are not told exactly what Adam's body was like, we may assume that it was similar to ours; a complex structure of cells, tissues, organs and systems that work together to sustain life on a physical level.

The spirit is that immaterial component of man which enables him to communicate with his creator. That man is more than just a complex system of electrochemical reactions is self-evident. He has a built-in *God*-consciousness and self-consciousness which enables him to perceive himself in relation to his creator. The spirit is what allows us to see ourselves in relation to God and others. It also provides us with a moral conscious for discernment between right and wrong.

The soul is produced by the interaction between the body and the spirit. It is roughly equivalent to the psychological concept of personality. The life principle of the spirit interacts with the physical body to produce a personal nature which is *both expressed and perceived in our relationships with others.* Included within the realm of the soul are the concepts of the mind, various needs, emotions, and the will. Since the soul is produced by the interaction of the spirit and body, its development will also be determined by both physical and spiritual factors (see Figure 2).

The structure of man presented here is only a model that may be useful in understanding ourselves and others as God's creations. *Human beings are exceedingly complex,* and certainly cannot be understood apart from divine revelation. Because we are able to identify the various parts of man as body, soul, and spirit does not suggest that we are able to obtain a complete knowledge of humanity. However, the model described in figure 2 may be useful in organizing our thinking concerning the nature of human beings. Viewing man as a three-part being guards against the tendency to minimize our problems and oversimplify their solutions. For instance, *problems that may appear to be purely spiritual in nature, may also have some personal and physical characteristics, as well as vice versa.*

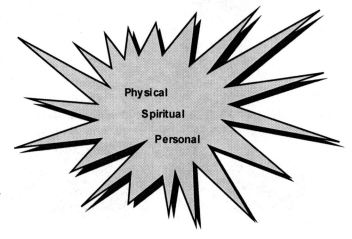

To the extent that we may begin to understand the complexities of ourselves as God's creations, we begin to be more impressed with our God. While humanistic philosophies and religions worship the creature (man) instead of the creator, the study of man from a biblical point of view is intended to ultimately im-

Alpha Series
Biblical Self-Awareness

Man cannot change or help himself

press us with the magnificence of God. Only an omniscient and sovereign creator could say that, "He needed not that any should testify of man; for he knew what was in man." (John 2:25). As the most complex of all God's creatures, mankind has a unique potential to reveal and glorify God as did the "Son of Man" during his earthly ministry. A truly biblical self-awareness will not only encourage us, but will also glorify God.

The preceding model of the structure of man helps to explain the difficulty inherent in confronting or changing the basic personality of human beings. The histories of our correctional institutions, rehabilitation programs, and mental hospitals reveal the inability of man to fully understand, much less change, himself. Only in the wisdom and strength of our creator can the human condition be altered. The good news is that God is, not only able, but willing to give us a brand new identity in himself. He, who originally created the universe, the earth, and the human race, will also provide us with an identity that is awesome in it's relationship to him. In love, he, who created all things, also calls us to himself as family. As we learn and receive by faith *who he has made us to be* we shall be able to say with confidence:

John 2:25

He needed not that any should testify of man; for he knew what was in man. (kjv)

"Because of Christ's redemption,

I am an awesome spirit-being

of magnificent worth as a person!"

Who Are You?

Alpha Series
Biblical Self-Awareness

QUESTIONS

CHAPTER ONE: BIBLICAL SELF-AWARENESS

Lesson One: Who Are You?

1. What kind of identities do we use to describe who we are?

2. What are the three images that relate to each one of us?

3. What is it about our own self image that is so important?

4. What three natures or components comprise the wholeness of man?

5. What is the purpose of each?

6. What should we remember about the relationship of these parts as we view problems?

BIBLICAL SELF-AWARENESS
FAMILY IDENTITY

Chapter 1
Lesson 2

The Biblical Foundations for Family Life

Since who we are as persons was determined in the physical realm by our family of origin, it is important to note the biblical foundations for family life. In the second chapter of Genesis we are given the story of how God created the family system. From the details of this record we discover how God intended for the family system to function, how the family reflects the full nature of God, and also, how the family became naturally dysfunctional.

The Divine Family

After God had created Adam, and met all his needs in the Garden of Eden, he states, "It is not good that the man should be alone: I will make a help meet for him." Notice, it was *God himself* who said it was not good for man to be alone. *Adam did not have a sense of loneliness* that might cause him to think of himself as being alone because he was in perfect communion with God. It was God who knew it was not good for man to reflect God's image and likeness as a solitary individual. Alone, Adam could not do it; it would be incomplete. It was *not good for God's purpose* in revealing himself through the creation of man, that Adam should remain alone.

Genesis 2:18

> *It is not good that the man should be alone; I will make a help meet for him.*

In order to fulfill his purpose in reflecting God's image *Adam had to enter into a family relationship*. The need for such a relationship was born out of the fact *God is a trinity revealed in family terms*. The Bible recognizes God the Father, God the Son, and God the Holy Spirit, as being one in essence (family), yet, three distinct persons. While the trinity is certainly a great mystery to our finite minds, the fact that it would take more than one person to accurately reflect the trinity should be apparent. Thus, God said it was not good for man to be alone. He must have a helper that was suitable for him to faithfully reveal the completeness of God, as well as to be fruitful and multiply, which further reveals his nature.

Through the creation of the woman, and ultimately children, God was revealing him-

Alpha Series
Biblical Self-Awareness

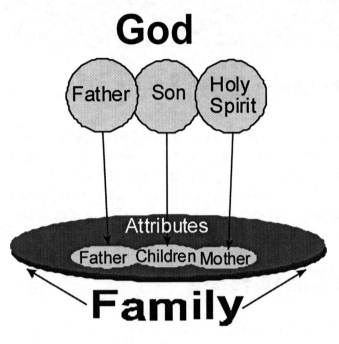

self as much in her, as he was in the creation of the man. Although the Bible constantly uses the masculine gender in referring to God, the divine being actually includes attributes that we think of as both masculine and feminine. Just as the terms, God the Father and God the Son, reveal the attributes thought of as masculine, the term, God the Holy Spirit, reveals the attributes thought of as feminine. References to the person and work of the Holy Spirit, in both the Old and New Testaments reflect the maternal and, therefore, clearly feminine attributes of God. Notable examples include the Spirit literally *"brooding" over the face of the deep*, in the original creation in Genesis 1:2. Also consider, those who are born again are *born of the Spirit* (John 3:1-8). Thus, the divine family of God the Father, God the Holy Spirit (mother), and God the Son, had to find expression beyond a solitary person. God created the family to express his attributes fully. For this reason God said it was not good for man to be alone. God needed a family.

Principles of Family Living

The unique manner in which God created the woman is significant in that it reveals what is required for *healthy family relationships* (Genesis 2:21-22). God did not make the woman from the elements of the earth as he did Adam, but, rather from Adam himself. God caused a deep sleep to come upon Adam. Symbolically, if not literally, this speaks of the fact that we must die to our natural self-centered life in order to relate to another. Such a death takes place when we receive Jesus Christ as our personal savior. In Adam's case, under a deep sleep he was literally cut in half. One-half of Adam was to become Eve. In our case, the old man (our old self, the self centered-self) is crucified with Christ, and a new man is raised up in its place that has the potential to love others like Christ loves them. Only those who have experienced the death of the old man are truly capable of healthy relationships.

The fact that God made the woman from half of Adam and then brought her to the man

Alpha Series
Biblical Self-Awareness

suggests that the woman was intended to be *different, but equal.* Much damage has been done to family relationships because the woman is *not recognized as totally different, but truly equal.* What makes her different is she was designed by God to respond to the initiative of her husband and not designed to assume leadership responsibilities. *She is in all respects equal in value and authority to the man, but has a totally different role in the family.* God brought the woman to the man to receive love, and to respond appropriately by returning respect. *Adam and Eve were made to compliment, rather than compete with, one another.*

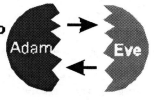

Another principle for a healthy family system is revealed in Adam's statement that the woman was, *"Bone of my bones and flesh of my flesh."* (Genesis 2:23) This simply means that the unity in marriage and family relationships is to be recognized as *so close it is considered oneness.* As a result, such a closeness, a oneness, means that it is impossible to hurt the other member, and get away without consequences. No matter how justified we may seem to be, we can never hurt another person without experiencing pain ourselves. In addition, we must also recognize that any opportunity to love and nurture another will also benefit ourselves. Through the making of Adam *and* Eve, God was giving the Golden Rule for family relationships. *One must die to self and live for the other.*

> **Genesis 2:23 - Oneness**
>
> *Bone of my bones, and flesh of my flesh* (kjv)
>
> The closeness of oneness
>
> One must die to self, and live for the other

The end of chapter two reveals *the ideal marriage relationship as being a spiritual, personal and physical oneness.* To experience this oneness requires us to first apply the gospel of who we are in Christ, to our own personal history, i.e. ...leave his father and his mother, and shall cleave unto his wife. Second, we must **maintain the goal of transparency**. This means we are honest with ourselves and our families about all issues of life. There can be no secret sins or hidden agendas that keep us from being real and honest with one another: "And

Family Identity

they were both naked, the man and his wife and were not ashamed." (Genesis 2:25)

The Attack On The Family

Anything God has established to reveal himself will immediately come under the attack of the enemy, and the family system is no exception! In the third chapter of Genesis, we are given the account of how the family system came under attack, and as a result, became dysfunctional. Although conditions in the Garden of Eden were radically different from those we experience today, the principles of temptation, and the resulting sin and dysfunction, remain the same.

> **An ideal family relationship:**
> 1. Lets go of the past conditioning of our family
> 2. Maintains the goal of transparency

Using the most intelligent animal God had made, Satan began the spiritual attack in earnest with a most deceptive, but deadly, question concerning God's word and his goodness: "Yea, hath God said, ye shall not eat of every tree of the garden?" (Genesis 3:1) Satan's question was meant to cause Eve to doubt God's provision and willingness to satisfy all her needs. *Essentially, the same question arises in our own minds when we doubt what God has given us in Christ is really enough to satisfy us completely.*

> **The attack strategy**
> 1. Lead to negative thinking
> 2. Focus on what we cannot have.

Thinking negatively, about her own needs, Eve quickly focused her attention on the forbidden fruit as an answer to all that was missing in her life. It seemed to be just what she needed to satisfy her physical, personal and spiritual needs. This kind of *deception* concerning what it takes to satisfy our needs *is the central issue and root of all dysfunction* in our family systems. As will be seen in later studies, it is believing we need something more than what God has provided to satisfy our needs that ultimately causes us to become selfish and dysfunctional in our relationships.

The attack of the enemy is always the same! Create negative thinking, and then focus on what is missing or out of reach..

Although the Bible is clear that Adam was not deceived in the same manner as was Eve (1 Timothy 2:14), *he certainly joined her in her dysfunction and sin.* It was not the fruit that he thought he could not live without, it was Eve! He, also, started to believe he needed more than God to satisfy his need: Eve. Could he survive without Eve? After all, she had eaten the forbidden fruit! All the while Satan was attacking the mind of his wife, Adam remained quiet and passive. Rather than risking rejection by taking the lead, Adam retreated in fear, and submitted to Eve. She had become his God.

The consequences of their unbelief and transgression of God's law were felt immediately, by both Adam and Eve. *For the first time, they experienced an overwhelming sense of worthlessness and shame.* Trying desperately to cover their own nakedness with fig leaves, Adam and Eve displayed religious pride in seeking to fix themselves and each other rather than trust God.

Genesis 3:7-10

> *Then, it was as if their eyes were opened. They realized they were naked, so they sewed fig leaves together and made something to cover themselves. Then they heard the LORD God walking in the garden during the cool part of the day, and the man and his wife hid from the LORD God among the trees in the garden. But the LORD God called to the man and said, Where are you? The man answered, I heard you walking in the garden, and I was afraid because I was naked, so I hid.* (ncv)

In the actual presence of a holy God, however, their pitiful efforts were not enough to save themselves; so they were terrified, and hid themselves. When questioned directly by God, they could no longer relate to one another. The beautiful marriage they enjoyed before had now become dysfunctional.

The Hope of the Gospel

It is against the dark background of personal and family dysfunction that the gospel is first introduced in the scriptures. Like a light shining in the darkness comes the hope of the good news of what God does for us to set us free from the bondage of personal and relational failure. The remaining verses in the third chapter of Genesis reveal the tender, but firm, manner in which God took the initiative to reach out to and save his dysfunctional family.

Genesis 3:15

> *And I will put enmity between thee and the woman, and between thy seed and her seed; it shall bruise thy head, and thou shalt bruise his heel."* (kjv)

The somewhat obscure promise of verse fifteen and the most beautiful picture in verse twenty-one are of particular importance in this passage. The enmity between the seed of the woman and the seed of the serpent speaks of the spiritual war between Christ and Satan over the dysfunctional human race. The fact that Christ will literally crush the head of the serpent reveals that God will ultimately restore to spiritual health all that was lost in Adam and Eve's fall. The personal application of this gospel is revealed in the fact that God, himself, made coats of skins to cover their nakedness (symbolic of dealing with their dysfunction with all its shame, fear, and pride). The glorious fact of the gospel is that God covers all our failure with the righteousness of Christ.

> **Genesis 3:21**
> *The LORD God made clothes from animal skins for the man and his wife and dressed them.* (ncv)

Throughout the lessons that follow in this series, we shall emphasize this one central theme of the gospel of Jesus Christ, and how it sets us free. As we learn and trust in all that God has done to make us new creatures in Christ, we are set free from our own fear, guilt and pride to reach out to others in true love. When each family member is assured of their own needs being met in Christ they are free to love one another with a divine love. Through our personal faith in who God made us to be in Christ, we have hope for ourselves. In the joy and confidence of our hope, we can actually love one another!

Alpha Series
Biblical Self-Awareness

QUESTIONS

CHAPTER ONE: BIBLICAL SELF AWARENESS

Lesson Two: Biblical Foundations for Family Life

1. Why did God say that it was not good for Adam to be alone?

2. What is God expressing in the family system?

3. When God caused a "deep sleep" to come upon Adam, what is represented symbolically?

4. How do the ideas of equality, similarity, and purpose pertain to men and women?

5. What is the chief consequence of not recognizing the reality of oneness?

6. What are two ways in which the ideal marriage relationship can be attained?

7. What is the central issue and root of all dysfunction in the family system?

8. What was the immediate result of the sin of Adam and Eve in the Garden of Eden?

9. What hope is expressed in Genesis 3:15 and Genesis 3:21?

Alpha Series
Biblical Self-Awareness

| FOUNDATION OF OUR NEEDS | Chapter 2 |
| JESUS MEETS OUR PERSONAL NEEDS | Lesson 1 |

Recognizing Our Needs

If we are going to really understand who we are, we must learn to recognize our needs *on a daily basis*. As a three-part being (body - soul - spirit) we have corresponding needs that must be met each day in order to live a healthy, functional life. In this lesson we will identify and define our basic needs, and then look at the manner in which God has promised to meet them with his gracious provisions.

Needs must be met daily

To help us understand our needs, we will divide them into three categories relative to the three components of man. The first of these needs is physical. Because we have a *physical body*, we obviously have a set of *physical needs* that must be met daily in order to continue living. Obvious needs such as air, food, and water fall into this category. Not as obvious, but also needed daily to continue living, is the need for the electrochemical balance within the body known as physiological homeostasis. This simply means that the various systems within the body are working together without disease or injury. For the purpose of this study, we shall summarize all our physical needs by the word **"health"**.

HEALTH

BODY
Physical Needs

Air

Food

Water

Physiological homeostasis

Second, in addition to our needs for physical health, we also must recognize the needs of our soul. We are more than just a physical being, therefore, we have more than just physical needs. As a soul or a person, we also have a set of personal needs that have to be met daily. *A common mistake in trying to understand our needs, is to overlook the fact that we actually have personal needs.* Because we are a person, we are going to have personal needs that must be met on a daily basis. We shall summarize our personal needs with the term **"worth."**

WORTH

SOUL
Personal Needs

Self-esteem

Positive self-regard

To be loved

Everyday we need to know that we are personally

Alpha Series
Foundation of Our Needs

TO LOVE

SPIRITUAL NEEDS

To love others as Christ did

worthwhile in order to live and function on a personal level. We may also refer to the need for personal worth as the need for self-esteem or positive self-regard.

Third, we must also recognize the fact that as spirit beings we also have a set of spiritual needs. This category of needs corresponds to our spiritual life and is best described as "the need to love others as Christ did." These spiritual needs always have to do with realizing our full potential in Christ to minister to others. We shall summarize our spiritual needs with the term **"to love"**. *It is important to make the distinction between our need to be loved (a personal need) and the need to love others (a spiritual need).* The latter is simply a need we have to give love rather than to receive it.

Psychologist, Abraham Maslow, suggested the idea that all our needs may be arranged by using a structured hierarchy which ranks them according to their order of importance. This means that certain needs (higher in priority) must be met before others can be addressed (lower in priority). *This ranking is based upon survival, that is, what is necessary to keep the person alive and well.* Borrowing from his hierarchy, we shall arrange the categories of needs we just described as shown in figure 1.

The physical needs for health are placed at the bottom of the hierarchy. We cannot continue to live without the proper nourishment of our bodies. Therefore, the most basic needs

Figure 1

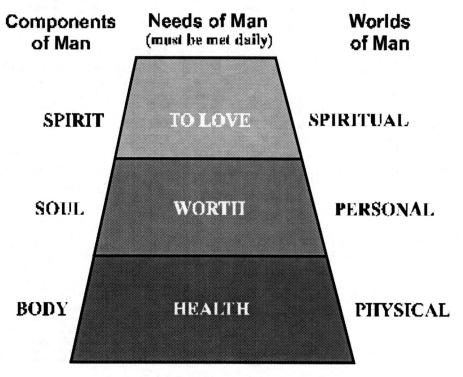

Alpha Series
Foundation of Our Needs

we have are those concerning our health. A man who is gasping for air or starving to death will simply not be concerned with personal worth issues. However, as the physical needs are met, then the personal needs begin to take priority in our lives. Likewise, when our personal needs are satisfied, our spiritual needs begin to take priority in our lives.

This order is important. It cannot be reversed. Spiritual needs cannot be met until both physical and personal needs are met. For instance, the importance of recognizing the hierarchical arrangement of our needs may be illustrated in family relationships. A husband and father who works hard to provide enough money for groceries, rent, gas, etc. *may think that he has met the needs of his family.* He brings home the paycheck expecting his wife and children to love and respect him for all that he has done. His unstated reasoning may be something like: "Because I have supported you with food and shelter, now you can at least, love and respect me enough to have dinner ready, and appreciate all that I have done for you."

> This order is important. It cannot be reversed. Spiritual needs cannot be met until both physical and personal needs are met.

Although Dad has met the physical needs of his family, he has overlooked the next level. He failed to understand his wife and children are more than physical beings. They have a set of *personal needs that must be also met* before they can exercise their spiritual need and give him any true love or respect. To make matters worse, Dad probably does not even realize he has a set of personal needs crying out to receive love and respect so loudly, that he is not really loving or respecting his family either. Dad must also have his personal needs met before he can exercise his spiritual need to love. Perhaps the single biggest cause for family strife and turmoil is the failure to recognize the importance of personal need satisfaction in our everyday lives. With everyone needing personal worth to be satisfied before their spiritual need (to love others) can be satisfied, are we not in a "Catch 22" situation? If no one can truly love another before being loved, where does it begin?

Personal Needs

In order to clarify our personal needs, we must expand our definition of the term "worth." The sense of personal worth that we need daily may be divided into *two categories: security and significance.* We need to know that we are secure and significant as persons. *First, security* comes from knowing we are *loved unconditionally,* without having to earn it or pay it back. *Second,* we need to know we are *accepted,* just as we are, without turning over a new leaf, or promising to do better. *Third,* we need know that we are *forgiven* for the past mistakes that continue to haunt our memories. Only when we know that we are loved, accepted, and forgiven, can we begin to experience true security

Alpha Series
Foundation of Our Needs

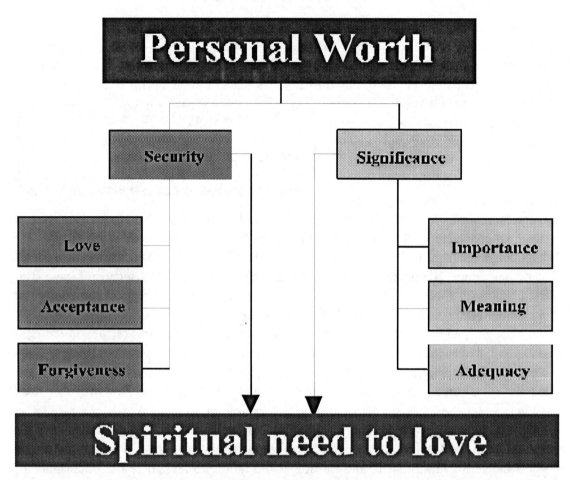

as a person. The other half of our personal need for worth may be summarized by the term "significance." *To experience personal significance requires knowing we are important, that our lives have meaning or purpose, and we are adequate to cope with our circumstances.* Taken together, the sense of importance, meaning, and adequacy make up our sense of personal significance. Together, **security and significance** determine our **personal worth**.

When we stop long enough to ask ourselves if these various needs are being met each day, most of us can think of a particular situation or circumstance that threatens one, or more of these needs. While the fact we are a person automatically means we have these personal needs, just being a person does not guarantee these needs will be met. In fact, the personal needs for most people, are not met on a regular basis. From the time we are born into this world we have been engaged in a daily struggle to meet these personal needs by our own means regardless of what it takes. Just as much as we need to eat food, our soul hungers for love. Just as surely as we thirst for water, our soul thirsts for significance.

For those who long to achieve the spiritual need to love, the personal hunger and

Alpha Series

Foundation of Our Needs

thirst in our souls must be satisfied before we can realize our potential to really care about, or love others as Christ. Only when our needs for security and significance are met can we go on to address the spiritual need to love and minister to others. We simply cannot give what we do not have. It is for this reason that we must turn our attention to *the true source of personal satisfaction*, our personal relationship with Jesus Christ.

The Bread of Life

One of the most difficult things for us to understand, regarding our personal needs, is how we get them freely and constantly satisfied on a daily basis. The story of Jesus feeding the multitude in the sixth chapter of the Gospel of John reveals some astonishing insight into our own struggle to trust Jesus Christ as our personal savior. While we may trust him as our

John 6:49-54

> 49 "Your ancestors ate the manna in the wilderness, and they died.
> 50 This is the bread that comes down from heaven, so that one may eat of it and not die.
> 51 I am the living bread that came down from heaven. Whoever eats of this bread will live forever; and the bread that I will give for the life of the world is my flesh.
> 52 The Jews then disputed among themselves, saying, "How can this man give us his flesh to eat?
> 53 So Jesus said to them, Very truly, I tell you, unless you eat the flesh of the Son of Man and drink his blood, you have no life in you.
> 54 Those who eat my flesh and drink my blood have eternal life, and I will raise them up on the last day;
> 55 For my flesh is true food and my blood is true drink.
> 56 Those who eat my flesh and drink my blood abide in me, and I in them.
> 57 Just as the living Father sent me, and I live because of the Father, so whoever eats me will live because of me.
> 58 This is the bread that came down from heaven, not like that which your ancestors ate, and they died. But the one who eats this bread will live forever. (nrsv)

Jesus Meets Our Needs

Alpha Series
Foundation of Our Needs

physical savior (and truly he is), relying upon him to provide for our physical needs; and we certainly trust him as our spiritual savior, relying on him to save us from hell; we find it difficult to trust him daily as our *personal* savior. The miracle that Jesus performed in feeding five thousand men and their families from one small boy's lunch was meant to demonstrate in the physical realm *what he is willing and able to do in the personal realm*. The multitude, however, missed the point and returned again the second day looking for another free lunch. Is Jesus just another free lunch for you? Do you come to Jesus as someone to give you material blessings? Or, do you come to Jesus for himself? Do you come to him for who he is? Do you come to him personally; trusting that in your relationship with him your personal needs will be satisfied? It was in this context that Jesus stated that he is the Bread of Life and, therefore, the only one that can truly meet all our needs.

The multitude had followed him to receive another meal. When Jesus exposed their true motivation for following him they became religious and sought to justify their preoccupation with their own physical needs by reminding him that God fed Israel daily in the wilderness with manna. In referring to himself as the "Bread of Life," Jesus was saying only by receiving him *personally* could they truly experience real life. He told them their ancestors who ate manna died, but those who eat this bread, the "Bread of Life" will never die (John 6:49-54).

While engaged in a heated discussion, Jesus made a statement that would shock them into understanding what he was really saying. He said, "Verily, verily, I say unto you, except you eat of the flesh of the Son of man and drink his blood, *you have no life in you*. **"Who so eats my flesh and drinks my blood *hath eternal life* and I will raise him up at the last day. For my flesh is meat indeed and my blood is drink indeed. He who eats my flesh and drinks my blood *dwells in me and I in him.*"** (John 6:53-54 - kjv)

By this, he meant only he could satisfy the hunger and thirst in their souls for personal worth. Only by becoming one with Jesus would they experience the personal security and significance they needed every day. Using a metaphor, in reference to eating his flesh and drinking his blood (apparent cannibalism), would certainly eliminate all who continued to think in physical terms only. Those who would eat and drink only of what this world offers for security and significance would never understand. However, for those who looked for more than just another free lunch (those who saw the obvious metaphor he was using)—these words offer tremendous hope by becoming one with Jesus. Whoever believes on him (i.e. eats his flesh and drinks his blood —consumes him —completely identifies with him) will enter into such a vital union with

> Is Jesus the Bread of Life
> or
> Another free lunch?

Alpha Series

Foundation of Our Needs

Christ that *whatever is true of Jesus is true of them as well.* The personal significance of such a statement, as understood in our union with Christ, is this: we are just as worthy as he is; we are just as secure as Jesus, himself. To accept Jesus Christ as our *personal* savior means we chose to believe we have become one with him; we chose to believe we are secure in his love and significant in his plan. It is trusting in our union with Christ that gives us a real sense of worth as a person and liberates us to realize our true potential in Christ to love others. *It is only then, when our personal needs are met, that our spiritual need to love others can be met.*

Alpha Series
Foundation of Our Needs

QUESTIONS

CHAPTER TWO: FOUNDATION OF OUR NEEDS

Lesson One: Jesus Meets Our Needs

1. What three needs do we all have and how do they correspond to the three components which constitute our being?

2. What is the ranking of needs and why is the ranking important?

3. Explain the categories involved in true personal worth.

4. What is the significance of Jesus being the "Bread Of Life?" (John 6:49-54)

5. How does Jesus work out the answer to question 4?

| FOUNDATION OF OUR NEEDS | Chapter 2 |
| OUR UNION WITH CHRIST | Lesson 2 |

In order to experience a true sense of personal worth, it is vital that we understand the very heart of the gospel message: *we have become one with Christ.* On the night before his crucifixion, Jesus sought to encourage his insecure and helpless disciples with a promise that reveals this gospel. He said, "At that day ye shall know that I am in my Father, and ye are in me, and I in you." (John 14:20) In this lesson, we shall focus our attention on the biblical basis for personal worth, as revealed in the promise of Christ that we are in him, and he is in us. In short, we shall examine our union with Christ as it applies to our personal needs.

The Promise

Before considering the exact meaning of our union with Christ, it is important to consider the context in which it was promised. The twelve had been following Jesus for about three years. They were trusting him to be the King of the Jews; the Messiah of Israel. Like all of us, they naturally believed that being with the King would give them personal worth. They were anxiously awaiting the day when Jesus would set up his kingdom on earth,

> **John 14:20**
> *On that day you will know that I am in my Father, and that you are in me and I am in you.* (ncv)

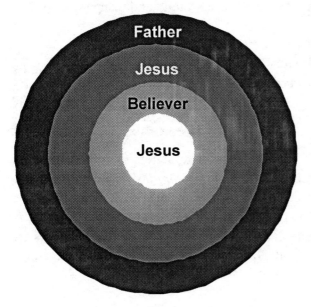

and they would receive prestige, money, and power by reigning with him. The fact they had left their natural ways and means of making themselves secure and significant would no longer worry them if Jesus would actually raise up his kingdom now. It was an investment to them.

Instead, Jesus told them he was leaving them now! All of their dreams and hopes for personal gain in the kingdom were crushed by this announcement. Immediately, they were overcome by feelings of insecurity and despair as the shocking news began to sink into their

Our Union With Christ

Alpha Series
Foundation of Our Needs

> "I am one with the father."

> It is this claim by Jesus that separates true Christianity from all other religions of the world.

> Because of our union with Christ we are worthy as persons.

> Because of our union with him we are secure and significant as persons whether we feel like it or not.

hearts.

It would be difficult to imagine a more desperate situation than the one facing those worried disciples that night. Clearly, they needed encouragement on a supernatural basis. Against such a background of darkness, shines the light of the gospel in Jesus' promise about their union with him. In contrast to the insecurity they naturally felt by the coming separation, the promise of their union with Christ offered comfort and joy for those who would believe. Likewise, only the promise of our union with Christ can truly comfort those who are feeling worthless.

John 14:20 states the promise Jesus made to his disciples concerning their union with him. Jesus' statement, "As I am in the Father" refers to his being one with the Father. It is this claim by Jesus that separates true Christianity from all other religions of the world. Jesus did not claim to be just another good teacher or prophet of Israel. He claimed to be God! Being "In the Father," means what is true of the Father is also true of Jesus because they are one in essence.

In exactly the same way he is in the father, Jesus promised his disciples (believers) they are in him. Whatever is true of Jesus being "In the Father," must also be true of the believer "In Christ." Thus, believers are one with Jesus just as he is one with the Father. In addition, he went on to promise *he is in the believer while the believer is in him.* The wonderful news is we are totally and inseparably joined to Jesus.

The concept of our union with Christ does not come only from this promise of Jesus. The Bible reveals the same truth through *different analogies.* Later Jesus would express the same promise to his disciples through the analogy of *the vine.* As the vine and its branches are one, so are believers one with

> Whatever is true of Jesus being " In the Father," must also be true of the believer In Christ.

Christ. The apostle Paul uses three different analogies in his letters to demonstrate the same promise. Believers are one with Christ as *a building and it's foundation* are one (Ephesians 2:20-22); as *a husband and wife* are one (Ephesians 5:31-32); as *the head and the body* are one (Ephesians 1:22-23). The frequent use of the phrases, *"In Christ," "In him,"* or *"In whom"* in the New Testament, all reflect the basic promise that believers are in a vital union with Jesus Christ. It is from this union the believer draws incredible benefits of personal worth.

Alpha Series

Foundation of Our Needs

The Benefits

Since Jesus' promise is true we can begin to realize the marvelous personal benefits of our union with him by reminding ourselves that what is true of Jesus is true of us as well. *Was Jesus secure in God's love?* Certainly he was, and *so are we*. *Was Jesus significant in God's plan?* Certainly he was, and *so are we*.

Because of our union with Christ we are worthy as persons. As we begin to recognize and believe in our union with Christ we enter into *the fullness of the gospel of Jesus Christ in our daily lives*. Because we are one with Christ (we are in him and he is in us) we are said to be loved unconditionally (Ephesians 2:1-10), totally accepted (Ephesians 1:3-6), forever forgiven (Colossians 2:9-15), important as ambassadors (2 Corinthians 5:17-21), meaningful in ministry (John 14:12), and adequate in power (Philippians 4:13). In short, our union with Christ meets all our personal needs to make us worthy *because he is worthy.*

We are:

Loved unconditionally	(Ephesians 2:1-10)
Totally accepted	(Ephesians 1:3-6)
Forever forgiven	(Colossians 2:9-15)
Important as ambassadors	(2 Corinthians 5:17-21)
Meaningful in ministry	(John 14:12)
Adequate in power	(Philippians 4:13)

It is necessary at this point to consider an important distinction between *being* worthy and *feeling* worthy. Jesus promised to be one with us to make us worthy; not necessarily to make us feel worthy. It is possible for us to *be* absolutely secure, and yet *feel* insecure. Carnival rides and amusement parks entertain people by causing them to experience a feeling of insecurity, while they really are secure. Jesus has promised to make us absolutely secure and significant in his love and calling regardless of what we may experience in our feelings. Because of our union with him *we are secure and significant as persons whether we feel like it or not.*

The Faith

In spite of the fact Jesus has promised to identify himself with us and us with him in order to give us a true sense of worth, there are many other things we have learned to depend on for our personal security and significance. Before we are old enough to abstractly conceive that there is a God at all, let alone one who loves us and gave his life for us, *we have all been conditioned to trust in ourselves, others, and our circumstances to make us worthy.* As

The Faith Factor

Our union with Christ

Alpha Series
Foundation of Our Needs

small children we learn to *trust in our own performance* to make us significant in this life. We also learn to *depend on the approval of significant others* to tell us we are loved, and, therefore, secure. These early learning experiences make it very difficult to later believe Jesus is the one who makes us secure and significant.

The multitudes turned away, and walked no more with Jesus (John 6:66) because they were not willing to believe that he could satisfy their personal needs by himself. When Jesus refused to give them another "free lunch," they, thinking only physically in their natural, pre-conditioned ways, could see nothing Jesus had to offer to get their needs met.

Each of us fight the same kind of battle today. When we honestly ask ourselves what we depend on for our worth (i.e. security and/or significance) we also find that we have been conditioned from birth to trust everything and everyone but Jesus. In our natural condition, what Jesus has to offer does not make any sense to us either.

For instance, suppose I bought a Lotto ticket, and won ninety million dollars. The money I would have won would generate a *false* sense of security as people begin to say they "love" me, they "accept" me, and they "forgive" me for any wrongdoing. Likewise, I might develop a *false sense* of significance as I enjoyed a new sense of "importance," "purpose," and "power" in my money. All my conditioning in this world's value system would tell me that I am now "worth" ninety million dollars. Trusting Jesus, rather than ninety million dollars for my worth, would be a great deal easier to *say* than to *do*.

As we shall see in later lessons, the factor that allows us to develop, and maintain a healthy sense of personal worth, is simply *faith in our union with Christ*. The reality is, as far as God is concerned, only those who are "in Christ" or "one with Christ" have any real worth as persons. For this reason he sent his son Jesus to identify himself with us in our worthless condition of sin that we might identify ourselves in his worthy condition of righteousness. *In Christ, we have all that is necessary to make us secure and significant.* Apart from Christ we have nothing. The only thing left for us to do is to believe. That is, we must chose to base our worth each day on our union with Christ (eat his flesh, and drink his blood, daily). "For by grace are ye saved through faith; and that not of yourselves: it is the gift of God: not of works, lest any man should boast." (Ephesians 2:8-9). It is by grace, through faith, that we are saved from eternal death (the condition we are already in because of our natural birth, and will stay in without being reborn from above). It is also by grace through faith that we are saved from the personal death of worthlessness.

Alpha Series
Foundation of Our Needs

BECUASE WE ARE ONE IN CHRIST
WE ARE:

Totally accepted (Ephesians 1:3-6)

Forever forgiven (Colossians 2:9-15)

Loved unconditionally (Ephesians 2:1-10)

Important as ambassadors (2 Corinthians 5:17-21)

Adequate in power (Philippians 4:13)

Meaningful in ministry (John 14:12)

Our Union With Christ

Alpha Series
Foundation of Our Needs

QUESTIONS

CHAPTER TWO: FOUNDATION OF OUR NEEDS

Lesson Two: Our Union With Christ

1. What is the significance of the promise Jesus gives in John 14:20?

2. Why does our union with Christ meet our personal needs and make us worthy?

3. What role does our faith play?

4. List the things mentioned that are true of us when we are in Christ.

UNDERSTANDING OUR EMOTIONS — Chapter 3
CATEGORIES OF EMOTION — Lesson 1

No attempt to examine ourselves is complete without understanding our emotions. Although difficult to objectively measure and define, emotions are obviously important to the quality of our personal and relational lives. In this lesson we shall describe the components and categories of emotions so that you may gain the necessary insight to effectively manage your feelings on a day-to-day basis.

Components of Emotions

At the risk of oversimplifying a complex subject, we shall divide our emotional experience into two main components, the physical and the mental.

The first is the physical component of our emotions, and involves all the physiological changes that occur in our bodies whenever we experience emotional arousal. We often refer to such changes in our bodies as "feeling" because we actually do feel them physically. That is, how strongly we *feel* an emotion is *directly related to the physical changes* within our bodies. The *feeling* is a *reaction* to the physical changes occurring.

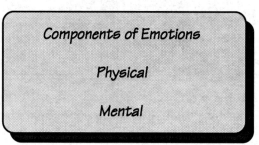

In his book, *THE STRESS OF LIFE*, researcher Hans Selye has identified a pattern of physical changes that occur when experimental animals are exposed to various kinds of stress. As illustrated in figure 1, the body naturally reacts to the stress-causing event in what he calls the *alert stage*. During this initial stage the autonomic nervous system

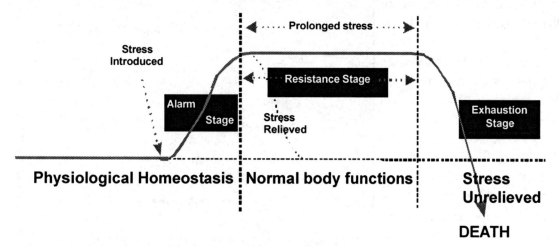

Alpha Series
Understanding Our Emotions

prepares the body by increasing the heart rate, blood pressure, and respiratory rate as well as causing many other changes necessary to cope with the stress. All of these physiological changes, which are normal and healthy, have the same basic goal: survival of the individual. When the stress is eliminated or relieved, the body usually returns to normal functioning.

During his experiments, however, Selye noted that as long as the stress continued, the body also continued to function in a constant state of arousal. He called this stage the *resistance stage*. During prolonged periods of stress the body would adapt to the stress by creating the physical changes noted in the alarm stage. However, such resistance carried with it a high cost. Sooner or later the body would move into the *exhaustion stage,* resulting in the death of the animal.

The negative effects of stress on the human body have long been seen by medical researchers as well. In his book, *NONE OF THESE DISEASES*, Dr. C. I. McMillian lists a wide variety of medical conditions people suffer as a result of prolonged stress in their lives. These ailments are referred to as psychosomatic disorders, and may range from simple skin rashes to intestinal symptoms such as ulcers. It has been estimated that one-half the people who are hospitalized are suffering from a psychosomatic ailment due to stress. Learning to cope with the emotional stress of everyday life is as important as learning proper nutrition or hygiene. Perhaps Jesus had this in mind when he told the Tempter that, "Man shall not live by bread alone, but by every word that proceeds out of the mouth of God" (Matthew 4:4).

> Matthew 4:4
> *Man shall not live by bread alone, but by every word that proceeds out of the mouth of God. (kjv)*

Important as the physical component of our emotions is, it seems only to account for the intensity of our emotions. The question remains, however, what is it that determines the quality of our emotions? What actually causes us to feel angry or depressed or anxious? The second, and perhaps the more important component of our emotions, is referred to as the cognitive, or mental, component. The mental component is the causal

PHYSICAL	MENTAL
Is a reaction	Is the causal agent
Produces feelings	Based upon beliefs
Determines intensity	Determines quality

(The greater the physical change, the greater the feeling)

Categories of Emotions

component of our emotions. While *the physical component determines the intensity of our feelings, the mental component determines the quality of our emotions, i.e. whether we feel joy, or rage, or hurt, etc.* When questioned about our feelings it is natural to assume that some particular event or situation has caused us to feel a certain emotion. For instance, we may say that someone "hurt" our feelings by what they said about us. We assume that our emotional hurt was actually caused by what was said, and completely ignore the cognitive component of those hurt feelings. The problem with this understanding is that it removes control of our feelings from us, and puts us at the mercy of whoever we let control our emotions. In order to regain control of our own feelings we must understand the cognitive component that decides the quality of our emotions.

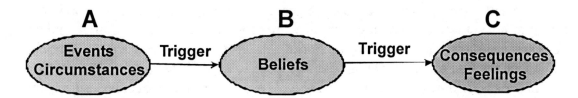

Psychologist, Albert Ellis, sheds some light on the mental component of our emotions in what is called the ABC theory. This theory states that it is not simply the events (A) that happen to us that produce certain emotional consequences (C). Between event (A), and consequence (C) lies our beliefs (B), which actually connect (A), and (C). In short, it is not just what happens to us that causes us to feel a certain way, it is also what we believe, and tell ourselves about what just happened to us that really determines how we feel. For instance, I may lose my job, and feel anxiety due to a lack of income. However, it is not the loss of my job, or the lack of income that is causing my anxiety, it is the beliefs that I am mentally processing about myself in light of losing my job that are actually causing me to worry.

Although the personal responsibility associated with the mental component of our emotions may seem to place an added burden on us at first, it is the real key to experiencing emotional freedom. Realizing my beliefs are causing me emotional stress may seem to add more stress initially. However, if I can understand that my belief systems determine the quality of my emotions, I can then work on correcting my beliefs to alter my emotional responses. I may not change the fact that I lost my job, but I can change what I am thinking and believing about myself in relation to losing my job. Changing our belief systems or "self-talk" is the subject of our next chapter. For now, we simply need to recognize the potential we have to control our own feelings by changing our beliefs.

Alpha Series
Understanding Our Emotions

Categories of Emotions

To help clarify our thinking about our emotions it is useful to categorize the various emotional states according to figure 2. Each term on the chart may be thought of as a category of emotional states. While other terms may be used to describe each category, these have been chosen to correlate with the biblical terms, and minimize semantic confusion. In addition, each category is headed up with a positive emotion (LOVE, JOY, and PEACE), and may be viewed as a degenerating range from complete love at the top to no love (HATE) at the bottom of the chart.

The positive emotions of love, joy, and peace are obviously ones that feel good. It is crucial to note, however, that these emotions are called the "fruit of the Spirit", and are therefore, *emotional states that **only** the Holy Spirit produces in us.* Since these emotions are, in fact, the fruit of the Spirit it is possible for us to experience love, joy, and peace *in spite of the circumstances* of our lives. A notable example is that of Paul and Silas being able to sing praises in the midst of their suffering in prison (Acts 16).

The opposite of the positive emotions are referred to as destructive or sinful, rather

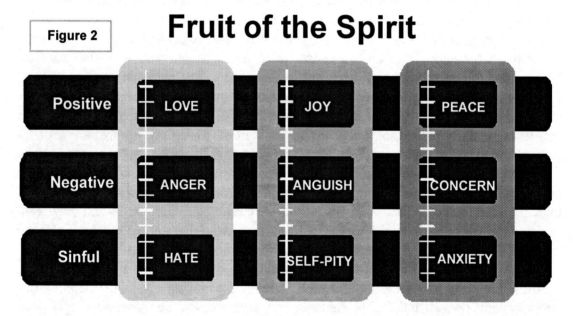

than negative, emotions. *Hatred, self-pity, and anxiety* are not sinful simply because God has arbitrarily decided to call such feelings sin, but because *such emotional states are destructive and lead us to death in some form.* These sinful emotions may produce *psychosomatic disorders* that bring on the death of a tissue, organ, or even the individual himself. Likewise, sinful emotional states lead to a relational death as they *destroy our*

Alpha Series
Understanding Our Emotions

> **Sinful emotions:**
> - Cause death
> - Limited death or poor health
> - Complete death of the person
> - Relational death

relationships to others. The Bible declares that anything leading you to death in any form is sin. "For the wages of sin is death" (Romans 6:23).

Somewhere between the positive and the sinful emotions are those feelings we may describe as negative. Negative emotions are not pleasant, but they do not produce death in us. Although they are obviously different from the positive emotions, they may be seen as including a measure of the positive emotions in them. For example, Jesus was obviously angry when he cleansed the temple during his public ministry, yet he still loved the merchants he drove out. It is possible to be angry, and not sin (Ephesians 4:26) since anger still contains a measure of love. Likewise, we may experience excruciating pain and anguish without feeling sorry for ourselves. Jesus' own agony in the Garden of Gethsemane is a classic example of pain that contains an element of joy or biblical hope. Finally, we may experience genuine concern for our own or other's welfare without becoming anxious or worried due to the "peace that passes all understanding."

> **Negative emotions:**
> - Are not sinful
> - Negative emotions have an element of the positive
> - Sinful emotions have no element of the positive

> **Ephesians 4:26**
> **Be Angry and Not Sin**
> *Be angry but do not sin; do not let the sun go down on your anger (nrsv)*

As our supreme example we look to Jesus who truly experienced all of the negative emotions in life yet was without sin (Hebrews 4:15). Most of his earthly life and ministry was not spent in some sort of blissful state of "love, joy, and peace." Rather he was "a man of sorrows, and acquainted with grief" (Isaiah 53:3) who, though he felt the negative emotions, maintained the love, joy and peace of the Spirit, daily, throughout his often difficult life. He did this by choosing daily to believe in who he was, and

> **Hebrews 4:15**
> **The Supreme Example**
> *For we do not have a high priest who is unable to sympathize with our weaknesses, but we have one who in every respect has been tested as we are, yet without sin. (nrsv)*

Categories of Emotions

Alpha Series
Understanding Our Emotions

trusting in the provisions of his heavenly Father. More will be said about coping with our emotions in the next chapter, but for now we must recognize that **the only way to stay away from death-producing sinful emotions is to exercise faith in the gospel that produces the fruit of the Spirit in our lives.**

Alpha Series
Understanding Our Emotions

QUESTIONS

CHAPTER THREE: UNDERSTANDING OUR EMOTIONS

Lesson One: Categories of Emotions

1. What are the two main components of emotions?

2. What is the result of prolonged and unrelieved stress?

3. What roles do the two main components play in our emotional states?

4. What links the circumstances and events of our lives to the feelings that result?

5. What are the three categories of emotions?

Alpha Series
Understanding Our Emotions

UNDERSTANDING OUR EMOTIONS — Chapter 3
EMOTIONAL HEALING — Lesson 2

Sinful emotions such as hatred, self-pity, and anxiety can destroy us personally, and our relationships with others. Although we naturally defend ourselves from such experiences through what psychologists call defense mechanisms (denial, projections, repression, etc.), these serve only to keep our rage, hurt, and worry out of our conscious awareness. The "bottled-up" emotions from past experiences will, sooner or later, find expression through psychosomatic disorders, personal dysfunction, and relational difficulties. In this lesson, we will begin to explore the ways we may cope with these sinful emotions.

From Hatred To Love

In Matthew 18 we find Jesus instructing his disciples about how to cope with the interpersonal strife brought on by jealousy and hatred. The occasion for this instruction was the question, "Who is the greatest in the Kingdom of Heaven?" Such a question from the disciples implies several things. First, it suggests the disciples were competing with one another in the natural effort to meet their own needs for worth. Second, their competition would eliminate any genuine love being displayed, and engender a great deal of bitterness and resentment. Finally, their hatred for one another would naturally lead to further strife and personal offenses.

Jesus began to teach his disciples by first giving them an object lesson on what it takes to achieve spiritual greatness in his kingdom. (Matthew 18:1-5). As he called a small child to himself and set him in the middle of those adult men, he told them

> *¹ At that time the disciples came to Jesus and asked, "Who is the greatest in the kingdom of heaven?"*
> *² He called a child, whom he put among them,*
> *³ and said, "Truly I tell you, unless you change and become like children, you will never enter the kingdom of heaven.*
> *⁴ Whoever becomes humble like this child is the greatest in the kingdom of heaven.*
> *⁵ Whoever welcomes one such child in my name welcomes me." Matt. 18:1-5 (nrsv)*

Emotional Healing

Alpha Series
Understanding Our Emotions

> *7 "Woe to the world because of stumbling blocks! Occasions for stumbling are bound to come, but woe to the one by whom the stumbling block comes!*
> *8 If your hand or your foot causes you to stumble, cut it off and throw it away; it is better for you to enter life maimed or lame than to have two hands or two feet and to be thrown into the eternal fire.*
> *9 And if your eye causes you to stumble, tear it out and throw it away; it is better for you to enter life with one eye than to have two eyes and to be thrown into the hell of fire.*
> *10 "Take care that you do not despise one of these little ones; for, I tell you, in heaven their angels continually see the face of my Father in heaven.*
> *Matthew 18: 7-10 (nrsv)*

they would have to become like this little child, and humble themselves in order to be the greatest. By this he meant they would have to let his love make them worthy rather than compete with one another to prove their worth. ***When we, in childlike faith, trust Jesus to make us secure and significant, we are on our way to spiritual greatness.*** It is not our competitive skills that make us great; it is our ability to let Jesus meet our needs that sets us free to be the greatest in the Kingdom.

In verses 7-10 of this chapter, Jesus uses some very strong language to teach us how we must handle the deception which keeps us from receiving our worth from him and loving others. He first gives a warning to those who offend others (verse 6). He knows that wounded people will wound others because of their own rage and bitterness. And so, he gives the stern warning that it would be better to die quickly by drowning rather than continue a life filled with hatred for others. Further, he pronounces a woe upon all those who offend others because of their own woundedness and the hatred festering in their souls (verse 7). Unless some drastic steps are taken toward healing the hatred within, wounded people will continue to offend others, and destroy their own relationships.

The real problem with offenses is not simply the outward behaviors of strife and bitterness. The real problem is the inward condition of hatred in the soul that produces those outward acts. *It is that inward condition that Jesus refers to in verses 8-10.* Through the use of very graphic language Jesus teaches us that we are going to have to experience a great deal of self-inflicted pain to eliminate the hatred that causes offenses. Using the analogy of cutting off one's hand or foot, and plucking out one's eye, Jesus reveals the drastic measures required to eliminate the hatred and bitterness of the soul that prompts us to offend others.

Alpha Series
Understanding Our Emotions

The self-inflicted pain Jesus is referring to in this passage is the pain that we must experience when we take a long look inside our souls. When we are disappointed or hurt by others we naturally react with resentment, bitterness and hatred. In our efforts to cope with such wounds we often simply repress the memories and all the emotions that were produced at the time we were wounded. Although we may be able to "go on with our lives"

> The self inflicted pain Jesus is referring to in this passage is the pain that we must experience when we take a long look inside our souls.

on the surface, deep inside our souls an abscess of hatred begins to form. It is those pockets of hatred inside that produce symptoms of personal dysfunction and relational problems. Unless we take the time to honestly examine ourselves, and face the painful memories that produced the hatred inside, we can never "enter into life" as Jesus said.

The term "hell fire" that Jesus uses in verse 9 should be understood in the literal sense of "Gehenna of the fire." The failure to endure the pain necessary to cleanse our souls of hatred will result in being cast into the "Gehenna of the fire" (the trash dump outside the city of Jerusalem). Figuratively, this speaks of the personal dysfunction and relational disasters that characterize a life filled with hatred, rage, and bitterness. Jesus is warning us to either deal with the abscess of hatred inside or trash our lives.

The actual process of eliminating the internal hatred that leads us to external strife is best described by the biblical concept of forgiveness. When we find ourselves hating those who have disappointed or abused us in some way, we must first admit that we are, in fact, hating. Getting honest with ourselves and God about our hatred is really all the Bible requires for cleansing. We need to recognize that our hatred toward others who have hurt us (including ourselves and God) is as much a sin as the wrongs that we have suffered. While it is true others were at fault for wounding us in some way, we must realize hating them is never justified in God's eyes. *Our fleshly response of hatred toward the offender will continue to destroy our lives long after the offense has ceased.*

> My hatred destroys me.

If anyone had a right to hate those who abused him, it was Jesus. Yet, during his crucifixion, Jesus prayed, "Father forgive them." *For us to do anything less than forgive those who wound us is ultimately dysfunctional.* However, we cannot give what we do not have. It is absolutely impossible for us to forgive others unless we know

> Anything less than forgiving those who wound us is ultimately dysfunctional.

Emotional Healing   49

Alpha Series
Understanding Our Emotions

we have received forgiveness ourselves. "But, why do I need forgiveness?" we might say to ourselves. "I am the victim here, others are the offenders!" We need forgiveness for the hatred we have in our souls for others who offend us. When we confess our hatred to God, he is faithful (every time) and just (because he has already paid the penalty) to send away our hatred, and cleanse our personal and relational lives(1 John 1:9). Then, and, only then, are we truly able to forgive others who trespass against us. Then, and only then, are we able to move from hatred to love for our enemies.

From Self-Pity To Joy

In the Garden of Gethsemane, Jesus, reveals the manner in which we may learn to cope with real pain, without becoming bitter and hateful. As he entered the garden Jesus experienced a shock wave of grief and astonishment (Matthew 26:36-45). How he dealt with his personal agony that night provides us with a helpful model for coping with ours.

First, it should be noted that *Jesus was willing to face his pain and be honest with the Father and others about it.* Our natural defenses will often seek to minimize pain through denial. But, Jesus honestly embraced his pain *without pretending* it did not affect him—he was honest with the disciples who were with him. In verse 38, he said, "My soul is exceeding sorrowful, even unto death: tarry

> **The Honesty of Jesus**
>
> Sit here while I go over there and pray."
>
> I am deeply grieved, even to death; remain here, and stay awake with me."
>
> My Father, if it is possible, let this cup pass from me; yet not what I want but what you want."
>
> So, could you not stay awake with me one hour?
>
> Stay awake and pray that you may not come into the time of trial; the spirit indeed is willing, but the flesh is weak."
>
> My Father, if this cannot pass unless I drink it, your will be done."
>
> Are you still sleeping and taking your rest? See, the hour is at hand, and the Son of Man is betrayed into the hands of sinners. (nrsv)

Alpha Series
Understanding Our Emotions

ye here, and watch with me." This open admission of his suffering is in strong contrast to the religious pretense of so many who deny their own hurt to avoid looking unspiritual. If we are going to learn to cope with pain we must learn to honestly face the pain without any pretenses whatsoever.

After honestly facing his own pain, and openly sharing that pain with others, Jesus fully acknowledged his agony to the Father. His words, "O my Father, if it were possible, let this cup pass from me," (kjv) reveal the intimacy he had with God that would allow him the freedom to be honest about his own feelings. This is especially true when our feelings run contrary to what God has called us to do or permitted to happen to us. We do not need to play religious games with God, pretending he does not know how we are really feeling. He knows! We need to fully express and admit openly our true feeling to him.

> **Isaiah 53:3-6**
> **Predicted Suffering**
>
> ³ "He was hated and rejected by people. He had much pain and suffering. People would not even look at him. He was hated, and we didn't even notice him.
> ⁴ But he took our suffering on him and felt our pain for us. We saw his suffering and thought God was punishing him.
> ⁵ But he was wounded for the wrong we did; he was crushed for the evil we did. The punishment, which made us well, was given to him, and we are healed because of his wounds.
> ⁶ We all have wandered away like sheep; each of us has gone his own way. But the LORD has put on him the punishment for all the evil we have done. (ncv)

In addition to fully admitting how he felt, Jesus immediately submitted himself and his suffering to the sovereign will of the Father. His statement, "Nevertheless not as I will, but as thou wilt." (kjv), demonstrates the highest faith possible. Jesus completely surrendered his own will into the hands of his Father because he fully trusted in his goodness regardless of the pain he suffered. Likewise, when we are willing to trust the Father's will, rather than our own, we will also submit ourselves to him. We will quit seeking to save our lives in favor of trusting his plan, even though it involves suffering and pain.

The personal benefits of giving up control of our lives to the heavenly Father are seen in Jesus immediately after his prayer. In his gospel, the physician, Luke, tells us Jesus' agony was so intense that he suffered the psychosomatic response of bleeding through his sweat glands. Following his prayer to the Father, however, angels appeared to strengthen him in the garden. Having received such comfort Jesus was able to return to his sleeping disciples, and actually minister to them in spite of his own agony. Because of his faith in the goodness and will of the Father, Jesus was filled with the joy that was necessary to free him to minister to his disciples.

However, the account of Jesus' agony in the garden is more than a beautiful example of how we may face our pain. It is actually the record of Jesus fulfilling an ancient prophecy concerning our suffering. In Isaiah 53:4, the prophet tells us that Jesus would actually bear our griefs, and carry our sorrows. The shockwave grief and astonishment Jesus submitted himself to in the garden that night was really all the pain of the human race. "O, my Father, if it were possible, let this cup pass from me." This cup, he could not avoid, held all the hurt we will ever experience. As Jesus experienced the full weight of our sufferings, it was so intense that his words, "My soul is exceeding sorrowful, even unto death." were not an exaggeration, but a true statement. Had he not submitted to his father's will, and received supernatural strength, our collective stress would have surely killed him, physically.

Because Jesus won the victory in the garden, he is referred to by the author of Hebrews as our High Priest who knows, by personal experience, all about our pain. "For we have not a High Priest which cannot be touched with the feelings of our infirmities; but was in all points tempted like as we are, yet without sin. Let us therefore come boldly unto the throne of grace, that we may obtain mercy, and find grace to help in time of need." (Hebrews 4:15,16).

From Anxiety To Peace

One of the most frequent phrases Jesus spoke to his disciples was, "Fear not." This tells us two things. First, the disciples were constantly filled with anxiety, like the rest of humanity. Second, Jesus was concerned to comfort the disciples with his own presence and power. Jesus' words of comfort and peace will be reserved for a later chapter. For now, we will focus attention on the formula for worry given in Philippians 4:6-9 (text quotes are kjv).

The apostle Paul offers three basic steps to dealing with the anxiety that seems to plague so many people today. Knowing that simple denial of the things we are anxious about will not be a workable solution, Paul first says, "Be careful for nothing; but in everything by prayer and supplication with thanksgiving, let your requests be made known to God." (verse 6.) The phrase "Be careful for nothing" is a command not to worry. It is not, however, a command to quit thinking. Many people suppose if they simply quit thinking about something, they will quit worrying about it. This simply is not true; since the subconscious mind is capable of thinking and worrying without our consciously being aware of it.

Instead of putting our worries out of our minds, Paul says we should turn those worries into prayers. Since we will naturally think about the things that worry us, he invites us to talk to God about them. Notice the word "everything" in that verse. We are to talk to God about everything that troubles us; no matter what it may be. As often as we think about whatever it is that worries us, we are to pray about it.

The promise in the next verse (verse 7) tells us of the supernatural benefit of turning our worry into prayer. "And the peace of God, which passeth all understanding, shall keep you hearts and minds through Jesus Christ." This means God will protect our hearts (subconscious minds) and minds (conscious minds) with the same peace that Jesus had. The reason it surpasses our understanding is that it has nothing to do with changing our circumstances. The peace, the world has to offer, depends on changing our circumstances; but the peace of God through Jesus Christ, comes as a fruit of the Holy Spirit regardless of our circumstances.

> **Philippians 4:6-9** — **Prescription For Worry**
>
> 6 "Do not worry about anything, but in everything by prayer and supplication with thanksgiving let your requests be made known to God.
> 7 And the peace of God, which surpasses all understanding, will guard your hearts and your minds in Christ Jesus.
> 8 Finally, beloved, whatever is true, whatever is honorable, whatever is just, whatever is pure, whatever is pleasing, whatever is commendable, if there is any excellence and if there is anything worthy of praise, think about these things."
> 9 Keep on doing the things that you have learned and received and heard and seen in me, and the God of peace will be with you. (nrsv)

Even though we may enjoy the peace that passes all understanding, unchanged circumstances frequently come back to haunt us later. For that reason, Paul goes on to instruct us to think positively. "Finally, brethren, whatsoever things are true, whatsoever things are honest, whatsoever things are just, whatsoever things are pure, whatsoever things are lovely, whatsoever things are of good report; if there be any virtue, and if there be any praise, think on these things." (verse 8). Receiving the peace that passes all understanding frees us to think positively about our circumstances. By nature, all worries have a negative cloud of doom covering them. The positive thinking about our circumstances lifts the cloud of doom so we may think even more clearly.

Thinking positive about our circumstances is not enough, however. The apostle goes one step further to tell us, "Those things, which ye have both learned and received and heard and seen in me, do" (verse 9). It is impossible to worry while we are actively

Alpha Series
Understanding Our Emotions

pursuing a plan. In order to quit worrying about our circumstances we are encouraged to do the things we know already. We may not know how to get out of certain difficulties, but in the meantime, there are always many things we already know we can do. Being actively involved with the things we know we <u>can</u> and <u>should</u> do helps keep us from worrying about the things we cannot change. A version of the serenity prayer may be a suitable summary for moving from anxiety to peace:

Lord, grant me the patience to accept

the things I cannot change

The strength to change the things I can

And the wisdom to know the difference.

Alpha Series
Understanding Our Emotions

QUESTIONS

CHAPTER THREE: UNDERSTANDING OUR EMOTIONS

Lesson Two: Emotional Healing

1. What is the significance of the way Jesus used the child in Matthew 18:1-5?

2. What is the significance of the inward condition that Jesus refers to in Matthew 18:8-10?

3. What effect does hatred have on the hater?

4. What is the key to overcoming hatred?

5. How do we move from self-pity to joy?

6. Where do we find Jesus giving a beautiful example of how to face pain?

7. How do we move from anxiety to peace?

Alpha Series
Understanding Our Emotions

THE HEART OF THE PROBLEM — Chapter 4
TRADITIONS OF MEN — Lesson 1

The biblical proverb, "as he thinketh in his heart, so is he...," illustrates the importance of understanding the operation of the mind. If we are going to understand, much less change, our behavior or feelings, we must examine the underlying thought processes of the mind. Since our thoughts determine the quality of our emotions and our feelings determine our behavior, it is important to clarify and, ultimately, change our thinking, in order to affect any lasting changes in our behavior.

The Mind

The concept of the mind may be best understood by dividing it into two components. The part of our minds that we are aware of at any given moment may be referred to as the conscious mind. This includes all the perceptions, thoughts, beliefs, attitudes, and reasoning that we are aware of during our waking hours. Although most of us would tend to deny that we talk to ourselves, research indicates that eighty-two percent of our brain activity involves speaking to ourselves in words and sentences known as "self-talk." Each day we talk to ourselves about how we relate to what we see going on in the world around us. What we say to ourselves reveals the way we view our place in our environment.

The second component of the mind is the part which is below our conscious daily awareness. Psychologists call it the subconscious mind because it operates beneath the surface of our personal awareness as illustrated in figure 1. We are normally unaware of what is going on in the subconscious mind. However, because the subconscious mind serves as a storehouse or reservoir of all our experiences, it

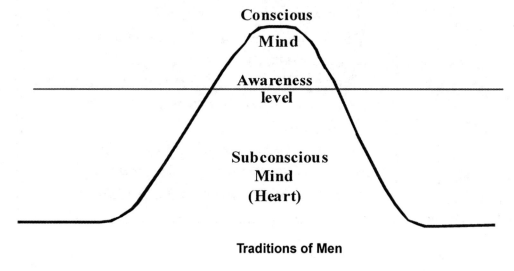

Traditions of Men

constitutes the greater part of our minds. Just as the greater mass of the iceberg is found beneath the water level, so also is the greater mass of the mind found below the awareness level. Included in subconscious mind are all the memories from past experiences regardless of their nature and all we have learned in order to survive and cope with life. The subconscious mind is the deepest part of our being, and, therefore, may be equated with the biblical concept of the "heart."

The Renewing of the Mind

The Bible is invaluable for shaping the heart and mind for personal growth and development. It is not simply a rule book for successful living, or a manual for emotional health. The written word is a revelation of the grace and truth of the Living Word, Jesus. It is meant to lead us to true repentance and faith. The word "repentance" comes from a compound Greek word (metanoia) which literally means "to change your thinking." Thus, the Bible is concerned with the renewing of the mind in order to effect lasting changes in our emotions and behavior.

In Ephesians 4:17-24, we are given a summary of the process involved in changing our natural state of dysfunction into a supernatural healthy state; and doing it from the inside out. The writer begins with a description of the need to change by telling us we are not to "live" (literally behave) like others who live (behave) "in the vanity of their minds." This last phrase of verse 17 refers to the emptiness

Eph 4:17-24 — **Changing your thinking**

> 17 *This I say therefore, and testify in the Lord, that ye henceforth walk not as other Gentiles walk, in the vanity of their mind.*
> 18 *Having the understanding darkened, being alienated from the life of God through the ignorance that is in them, because of the blindness of their heart:*
> 19 *Who being past feeling have given themselves over to lasciviousness, to work all uncleanness with greediness.*
> 20 *But ye have not so learned Christ;*
> 21 *If so be that ye have heard him, and have been taught by him, as the truth is in Jesus:*
> 22 *That ye put off concerning the former conversation the old man, which is corrupt according to the deceitful lust;*
> 23 *And be renewed in the spirit of your mind;*
> 24 *And that ye put on the new man, which after God is created in righteousness and true holiness (kjv)*

Alpha Series
The Heart of the Problem

of dysfunctional thinking, of both the conscious mind and the subconscious mind, and is further described in verse 18. The natural state of mind is dysfunctional because of confusion (darkened understanding), dissatisfaction due to ignorance, and the inability to live in reality (hardness of heart).

Such dysfunctional thinking will naturally produce serious emotional and behavioral problems which are described in verse 19. "Being past feeling" refers to the overwhelming flood of sinful emotions which simply cast aside all good intentions in favor of doing anything to make one feel good. In other words, when hatred, self-pity, and anxiety have become so intense that we can no longer stand it, we forget everything else and naturally set a goal to feel good at any cost. When the single most important thing in our lives is to feel better, we have given ourselves over "unto lasciviousness, to work uncleanness with greediness." We become totally self-centered and obsessed with making ourselves feel better regardless of what the long term consequences may be.

The New Man
- Taught the truth in Christ
- Renewed in the spirit of his mind
- Clothed with the new self
- Created according to the likeness of God
- In true righteousness and holiness (worthiness)

The natural man
- Futile thinking
- Darkened understanding
- Alienated from the life of God
- Ignorant
- Hard of heart
- Lost sensitivity
- Licentious
- Greedy
- Practices every kind of peerversion

With a note of reassurance concerning our true identity in Christ, the writer goes on to describe the biblical process of becoming healthy and functional. By personal experience with Jesus Christ we can learn there is a better way to live. As the truth concerning our worth in Christ is understood and believed, we are able to shed the naturally corrupt life-style of emotional and behavioral dysfunction. The critical step is emphasized in verse 23 which reveals we must be "renewed in the spirit of your minds." This means there must be renewed thinking (consciously and unconsciously) that will free us to take on a brand new identity (clothe yourselves with the new self) in Christ. The psalmist summarized this process when he cried out "Create in me a clean heart, O God; and renew a right spirit within me." (Psalm 51:10).

Psalm 51:10

Create in me a clean heart, O God; and renew a right spirit within me.

Alpha Series
The Heart of the Problem

The Traditions of Men

The renewal of our minds is a necessary process because our hearts are filled with the "traditions of men," rather than the truth of the Word of God. By "traditions of men" we mean the natural humanistic world view conditioned into each of us as we grow up. Later studies will fully demonstrate why these traditions are fundamentally wrong. For now, it is sufficient to note how Jesus exposes them as being the root cause of all our problems.

In Matthew 15:1-20, we find an account of Jesus in conflict with the religious leaders of his day. It was not unusual for him to be embroiled in a heated controversy involving the tradition of men. His entire message to the nation was summarized in one word, "REPENT," —change your thinking that has been encrusted with the traditions of men. So we find him again in controversy because his disciples violated the traditions of the elders when they failed to wash their hands before they ate bread (verse 1-2).

Jesus' response to the accusations of the religious authorities was to simply divert attention to the real problem. A problem which existed with them then, and now with us. He pointed out that our traditions themselves tend to violate commands of God, and can, therefore, cause us more damage by keeping them than by violating them. The specific example he used to illustrate his point concerned the way in which the traditions of the elders allowed for refusing to care for aging parents, if one had given all his extra money to the temple. Such a tradition permitted the Pharisees to avoid their family responsibilities before God, and still appear righteous before man.

> 1 *Then some Pharisees and teachers of the law came to Jesus from Jerusalem. They asked him,*
> 2 *"Why don't your followers obey the unwritten laws which have been handed down to us? They don't wash their hands before they eat."*
> *Matt 15:1-2 (ncv)*

Such hypocrisy brought to mind Isaiah's prophecy concerning the real problem we human beings have with our traditions. He said "This people draweth nigh unto me with their mouth, and honoreth me with their lips; but their *heart* is far from me." (emphasis added). The problem with our natural understanding of how we ought to live and function in a healthy way is that our "hearts" are miles away from God. Instead of knowing and sharing God's heart, we find ourselves in all sorts of denominational and traditional bondage; "teaching for doctrines the commandments of men." (verses 7-9)

Alpha Series
The Heart of the Problem

To bring his point home Jesus returns to the issue of failing to keep the tradition of the elders by not washing. To the multitudes, he made the radical statement that it is really not what goes into a man that defiles him, but rather what comes out of the man. *The dysfunction or defilement of sin does not come about by eating or drinking or drugging.* It is not what goes into the body that defiles the person. True dysfunction (defilement) arises because of what is already in us that comes out (verse 11).

> *"teaching for doctrines the commandments of men."*

This statement was so radical that Jesus' disciples were afraid Jesus had offended the authorities, and they would suffer because of it. To fully appreciate their fear, we must realize many of these traditions concerned the dietary laws given by Moses in the first five books of the Old Testament. Certain foods were strictly prohibited by the written law of God, and Jesus appeared to be contradicting them by his last radical statement.

After assuring his disciples that *the religious authorities were "blind leaders of the blind,"* and encouraging them to "let them alone," Jesus went on to explain what causes us to become dysfunctional. It is not the things we eat or drink (the things we do). The real source of defilement is what naturally comes out of our heart or subconscious mind. The prophet Jeremiah warns the heart is "desperately wicked and deceitful above all things," and contained in it is all the "evil thoughts that lead to murders, adulteries, fornications, thefts, false witnesses, blasphemies. . ." It is the "evil thoughts" springing up from within our subconscious minds that defiles us, and causes both personal and relational dysfunction in our lives (verses 15-29).

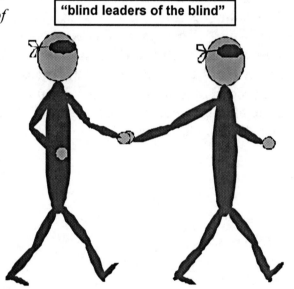
"blind leaders of the blind"

As a closing note in this study, let us define "evil thoughts" in terms more easily understood, and applied to our lives. An evil thought has at its core the idea —"I will be worthy if . . ." Regardless of how we may complete the sentence, the thought is evil. It is evil, because according to the gospel of Jesus Christ we've studied so far, it is a lie. To say "I will be worthy if . . ." implies we are right at this moment *worthless*, but if we can obtain something (whatever follows the if) we will be worthy. Continuing this further, it ultimately means we need something more than what God has already provided for us in Christ. *This is the core of the evil thought.*

Alpha Series
The Heart of the Problem

To see the evil character of such thinking, we have only to realize that when we think, "I will be worthy if . . .," we are really *calling God a liar, and rejecting Christ* as being sufficient to make us worthy. Instead of believing God has joined us, inseparably, to his son Jesus Christ, we may choose to believe that we must have someone or something more than what God has given us in Christ to make us worthy. It is this evil thought springing up in our hearts that actually defiles us and, underlies all our dysfunctional emotions and behavior.

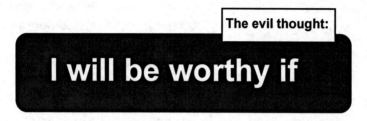

The core issue of all our problems is this: we do not, by our very nature, believe we are worthy (i.e. secure and significant) because of Christ. *The evil thought, "I will be worthy if . . .," betrays our real motivation every time.* This evil thought, in all forms, must be recognized and challenged in our minds. The truth of the gospel says, "I am worthy (i.e. secure and significant) because of who God has made me to be in Christ!" The process of replacing the natural evil thoughts with the gospel message is the renewing of the mind we all so desperately need. May our God grant us the grace to be changed each day from the inside out.

Alpha Series
The Heart of the Problem

QUESTIONS

CHAPTER FOUR: THE HEART OF THE PROBLEM

Lesson One: Traditions of Men

1. What are the two components of the mind?

2. What kind of thinking characterizes the natural mind?

3. What kind of thinking characterizes the New Man?

4. In understanding the "renewing of our minds," upon whom do we depend to do this?

5. What is the core problem with the traditions of men?

6. What is the evil thought that proceeds out of the heart?

Alpha Series
The Heart of the Problem

| THE HEART OF THE PROBLEM | Chapter 4 |
| HOW PROBLEMS DEVELOP | Lesson 2 |

In this lesson, we will combine all we have studied in previous lessons in a flowchart that describes how problems develop in our lives. In so doing, we hope to gain some practical insight into what is needed to be able to apply the gospel of Jesus Christ to our everyday lives. Living by faith in the gospel will not only improve the quality of our personal lives, but will also prepare us to relate to others in a functional, and more satisfying way.

At first glance, the flowchart page 71 appears to be very complex, but it is really somewhat over-simplified. The proper use of this chart requires a willingness to look at ourselves, rather than to judge others, and to allow the Holy Spirit to gently, but firmly, teach us what he will. Please do not attempt to use this flowchart as a club to force others into changing; but rather, use it as a mirror to identify your own need to change. When sharing it with others, your personal experience, given in a spirit of true humility, will go far to encourage, rather than intimidate, the listener.

The Solomon Syndrome

Deficit Motivation

The place to begin is in the very middle of the chart with the hierarchy of needs. Notice that both the physical and personal needs (health and worth, respectively) create in us a drive called deficit motivation. We identify deficit motivation as the drive to satisfy or fulfill whatever we believe is missing in our lives (the deficit). In the case of physical needs, we refer to the deficit motivation, that arises due to a lack of food or water, as "hunger" and "thirst." We are driven to meet our personal needs with the same kind of deficit motivation so that we may "hunger" for love and "thirst" for significance. As a matter of fact, Jesus identified our need for personal worth by using those very terms.

Hierarchy of Needs (Spiritual/To Love, Personal/Worth, Physical/Health) → **Deficit Motivation** → **False Assumptions** *I will be worthy if...*

How Problems Develop   65

Alpha Series
The Heart of the Problem

False Assumptions

Experiencing deficit motivation for worth as a person is common to all people. Every day we wake up with a hunger and thirst for worth because everyday we wake up as personal beings. Problems do not arise simply because we have deficit motivation. Problems begin when we naturally channel that deficit motivation through our versions of false assumptions, based upon —**"I will be worthy if. . ."** As you remember, these are the evil thoughts Jesus spoke of in Matthew 15 that defile a man. They are the traditions of men through which we ultimately violate the Word of God. When deficit motivation is channelled through the false assumptions of our heart (subconscious mind) we become selfish in our thinking, and all our behavior is self-centered.

Self-Centered Behavior

Self-centered behavior can often look quite altruistic, or religious, on the surface. We may do a variety of good works, and appear to be sacrificially giving of ourselves to others; and yet, really be looking for the praise and recognition of men. Any behavior based upon the false assumption **"I will be worthy if I do this or that"** is naturally self-centered. Even acts of kindness toward others, when motivated by the false assumption that "I will be worthy if...," are selfish in nature.

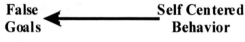

False Goals

All behavior, including self-centered behavior, is directed toward reaching some goal. Behavior is stimulated by the need or desire for some goal. In the case of self-centered behavior we identify the goal as being false. A false goal may not be necessarily "bad" in itself. **A goal is false because it cannot truly satisfy the need it is based upon.** For instance, doing nice things for people is not necessarily wrong by itself. However, it is wrong when doing nice things for people is motivated by the false assumption, "I will be worthy if other people approve of me" so I better do nice things for people. This is true not only because of the false assumption which underlies the false goal, but also because reaching that goal will only provide a temporary sense of satisfaction.

66   How Problems Develop

Alpha Series
The Heart of the Problem

Temporary Satisfaction, And a Vague Sense of Emptiness

False goals, that cause us to perform seeking the approval of others, always provide only a temporary sense of satisfaction. We seem to have an insatiable desire for better, bigger, nicer, etc. Regardless of how much success we achieve, we need more! **Regardless of how much applause we receive we naturally look for more.** The real problem with reaching a false goal is that, sooner or later, we experience the vague sense of emptiness that motivated us in the first place. We come, full circle, back to our personal need for worth, and the cycle starts all over again. False goals can only provide a temporary sense of satisfaction.

In the Book of Ecclesiastes, King Solomon gives us his testimony concerning the endless search for worth. The first two chapters detail the various things he tried to make himself worthy. His list of false goals includes: education, recreation, alcoholism, workaholism, sexual pleasure, relationships, politics, entertainment, fame, and wealth. His sad conclusion was, *"Vanity of Vanities, all is vanity, and vexation of spirit."* In other words, Solomon testified, that after trying everything, none of those things could truly satisfy his personal needs. He became suicidal as he despaired of life. **It is the vicious cycle of temporary success —trying to do, trying to be, and have everything under the sun to make us worthy— followed by emptiness, we call the Solomon Syndrome.** Most of the "American dream" is nothing more than trusting everyone other than Christ to satisfy our personal needs for worth. As a nation we are trapped in the Solomon Syndrome.

Hitting The Bottom

People in the recovery movement often talk about "hitting the bottom" as necessary to begin a course of recovery. Looking at the bottom of the chart we wonder why "hitting the bottom" seems necessary when we encounter various obstacles that keep us from reaching our false goals. Anything that prevents us from reaching our false goals will also be the source of tremendous frustration. "Hitting the bottom" may be seen as the build up of intense frustration after repeatedly hitting an obstacle that keeps us from reaching our false goals.

The frustration we experience when we encounter an obstacle will be expressed emotionally in one of three ways depending on the nature of the obstacle itself. If the obstacle is an external circumstance over which we have no control, then the frustration will be experienced as resentment or hatred. If the obstacle happens to be that our false goal is unreachable (i.e. perfection) then the frustration produced will be in the same dimension as self-pity. If the obstacle is simply the fear of failure ("I might fail if I try, and look bad; so I won't try"), then the frustration will be felt as anxiety. Hatred, self-pity, and anxiety are the three sinful/destructive emotions that lead us to many forms of death.

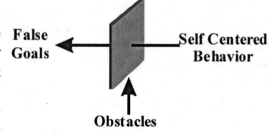

After repeated attempts to overcome the obstacles, the frustration is so intense that our health needs become threatened, and we must begin to deny, distort, or even break with reality. It is here that we may experience a personal death psychologists call neurosis or psychosis. "Hitting the bottom" is usually required before we call out for help, and seek a better way to live and function. It is when we are caught in this vicious cycle of repeated attempts to reach a false goal ending in frustration, that we are willing to do whatever is necessary to get help.

How frustration is experienced

1. Unreachable goals --------------------> Self-pity

2. External circumstances --------------->Resentment

3. Fear of failure -----------------------> Anxiety

However, the help we usually want is whatever we think we need to get past our obstacles, and reach our false goals. Many apparently unanswered prayers are accounted for when we understand we have been pleading with God to help us reach a false goal. Likewise, the counsel we seek, and the advice we think we need, are designed to help us get over, around, under, or through the obstacle that is keeping us from our false goal. We view anything less than reaching our false goal as inadequate or irrelevant.

Alpha Series
The Heart of the Problem

The Truth Shall Set You Free

The biblical approach to dealing with our obstacles is radically different from the secular. The Bible calls us to repentance; to change our thinking. In terms of the Solomon Syndrome chart, we are called to do two things:

1. Recognize our false goals are based upon false assumptions about our worth.

2. Replace those false assumptions with biblical assumptions.

Rather than continuing to strive for our false goals, we need to stop, and evaluate the false assumptions upon which those goals are based. *Every time we experience one of the emotions that leads to death (hatred, self-pity, anxiety), we know there is a false assumption and a false goal involved somewhere.* They need to be identified and evaluated. *Why should I work so hard to overcome such obstacles in an attempt to reach a false goal to make myself worthy, when God says I am already worthy?* Reflecting on this question is the key to changing our thinking, i.e. repentance. When we change our false assumptions, based upon "I will be worthy if . . . ," to the biblical assumption, "I am already worthy because of Christ," we have actually repented; we have changed our thinking, and chosen to believe the gospel of Jesus Christ.

To those who believed on him Jesus, said, "If ye continue in my word, then are ye my disciples indeed; and ye shall know the truth, and the truth shall make you free." (John 8:31-32). The truth Jesus was talking about is the biblical assumptions concerning our worth in him. When we believe the gospel that we are worthy because of our union with him, we are free to enter into a new lifestyle of grace and truth. The top of the chart diagrams the manner in which the truth sets us free to engage in Christ-centered behavior toward the true goals of ministry resulting in eternal satisfaction, rather than temporary satisfaction. An enhanced sense of worth frees us to concern ourselves with our spiritual need; expressing the love of Christ to others. While we will still encounter obstacles, the frustration we feel will be radically different... we experience negative, rather than sinful emotions. Our suffering with these obstacles will not lead to personal death, but rather to spiritual maturity in

Neurosis
Distortion and denial of the truth

Psychosis
Complete break with reality

How Problems Develop

Alpha Series
The Heart of the Problem

Christ. May God grant us the grace we need to identify, and reject the false assumptions, and replace them with the biblical assumption of our worth.

> *If ye continue in my word, then are ye my disciples indeed; and ye shall know the truth, and the truth shall make you free. (kjv)*

Alpha Series
The Heart of the Problem

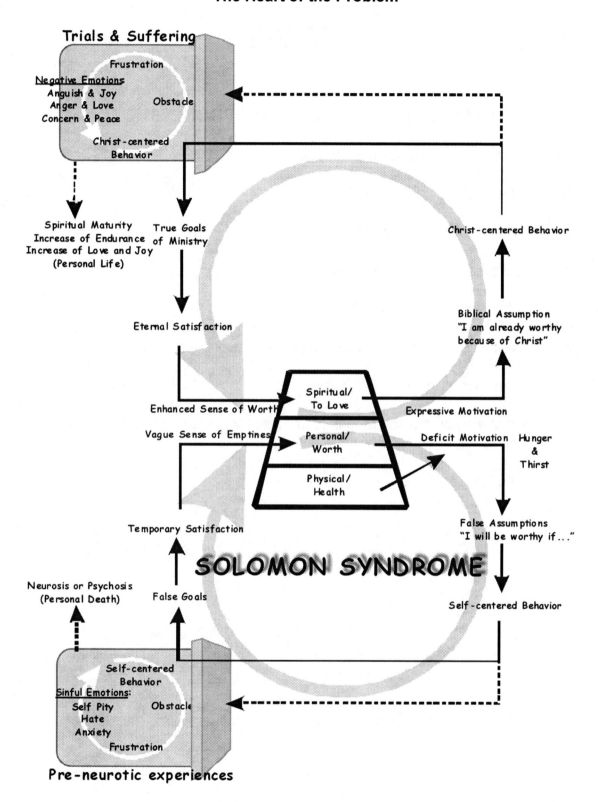

How Problems Develop

Alpha Series
The Heart of the Problem

QUESTIONS

CHAPTER FOUR: THE HEART OF THE PROBLEM

Lesson Two: How Problems Develop

1. What is deficit motivation?

2. What are false assumptions?

3. Describe self-centered behavior?

4. Why is a false goal false?

5. What is the problem with temporary satisfaction?

6. What is the Solomon Syndrome?

7. What are some of the results of encountering obstacles to achieving false goals?

8. What is the solution?

OUR TRUE IDENTITY — Chapter 5
GOD'S REGENERATION PROGRAM — Lesson 1

In the last study we learned the core issue of our personal problems is traced back to the false assumptions we hold concerning what it takes to make us worthy. Seeking to meet our needs for security and significance by anything other than the provisions of God in Christ will ultimately lead us to personal dysfunction. *Through repentance and faith we change our false assumptions to the biblical assumption "I am worthy in Christ."* Only then will we be able to live a truly functional life.

In this study we will begin to describe those biblical assumptions we are to believe concerning ourselves. Our goal is to lay the foundation upon which all biblical assumptions will be built in our minds. Since the false assumptions are so natural to us it is very difficult to even recognize, much less trust, the biblical assumptions concerning our worth. For this reason we shall focus our attention on the gospel of Jesus Christ as revealed in the book of Romans.

Romans 3:10-18

Human Nature

> 10 As the Scriptures say: "There is no one who always does what is right, not even one.
> 11 There is no one who understands. There is no one who looks to God for help.
> 12 All have turned away. Together, everyone has become useless. There is no one who does anything good; there is not even one.
> 13 "Their throats are like open graves; they use their tongues for telling lies. Their words are like snake poison.
> 14 "Their mouths are full of cursing and hate.
> 15 "They are always ready to kill people.
> 16 Everywhere they go they cause ruin and misery.
> 17 They don't know how to live in peace.
> 18 "They have no fear of God. (nrsv)

Alpha Series
Our True Identity

The Need For The Gospel

In the first two and one half chapters of Romans the apostle Paul proves that all people are in need of the gospel of Jesus Christ. In Romans 3:10-18 he gives us a very vivid description summarizing the character of the human nature apart from Christ. Using a series of references from the scriptures themselves, he systematically proves there is no one in the world that can lay claim to righteousness in himself. Further, he argues that no one understands or seeks after God and, instead, all have moved away from God, and have become corrupted. Finally, not one person in all the world is practicing kindness in himself. Basically, the natural condition of all people is totally self-centered and worthless.

Again using selected references from the Old Testament, Paul offers a word picture of the basic anatomy of our depraved nature, (verses 15-18). He describes the throat, tongue, lips, and mouth, (all organs of speech), as being filled with corruption, deceit, poison, cursing and bitterness. In addition, he describes the "feet" and "ways", (overt behavior patterns), as quickly hurting others, and leading to personal destruction and misery. Finally, he states that all men are ignorant of how to achieve true and lasting peace, and lacking any reverence or appreciation of the holy and righteous Creator. With this closing statement *all persons are found to be not only guilty, but also helpless to do anything about their condition.*

The natural condition
No one can claim to be righteous in himself
No one understands or seeks after God
All have moved away from God
All have become corrupted
No one is practicing kindness in himself

Natural Behavior patterns
Quick to hurt others
Personal destruction
Misery

Speech
Corruption
Deceit
Poison
Cursing
Bitterness

Not by law; but by faith — *Galatians 2:16*

Yet we know that a person is made right with God not by following the law, but by trusting in Jesus Christ. So we, too, have put our faith in Christ Jesus, that we might be made right with God because we trusted in Christ. It is not because we followed the law, because no one can be made right with God by following the law. (ncv)

Alpha Series
Our True Identity

The purpose of the law

That *"every mouth may be stopped, and all the world may become guilty before God."*

Shows us how helpless we are

We are incapable of reaching God's standards

Although this message seems rather blunt and even harsh, it serves a vital purpose in that *it reveals the desperate need for a personal savior.*

Continuing, Paul tells us the purpose of the law. It shows us how helpless we are, and in so doing, drives us to conclude we cannot possibly save ourselves, (verses 19-20). He equates the Old Testament scriptures with the law, and views them as applicable to all. He describes the law as continually speaking to all men for the purpose that *"every mouth may be stopped, and all the world may become guilty before God."* The logical conclusion from a careful study of the Old Testament scriptures is that human efforts are incapable of reaching God's standards of righteousness. Paul states that it is absolutely impossible for anyone to be justified (made righteous) in God's sight by his own efforts to keep the law. In other words, the law was not given so we may be justified by keeping its standards, but rather we might realize our utter helplessness and bondage to sin, and see our need for a savior (see also Galatians 2:16, 3:10-11,19-24). Now the stage is set for the revelation of the "good news" of what God has done for us in Christ that we were unable to do for ourselves.

Receiving God's Righteousness

In contrast to our worthless and helpless condition of sin, Paul goes on in verses 21-28 to describe how *God makes us worthy by giving us His righteousness as a gift.* The righteousness of God should be understood as righteousness which never has sinned, is not now sinning, and never will sin. It is the state of having always done what is right, never making a mistake. It is obvious that such righteousness *cannot be earned* by we who are *by nature s*inful and dysfunctional. Even if it were possible for us to turn over a new leaf, and rid ourselves of all sin in the future we could not match the righteousness of God which never has sinned.

It is clear we need that kind of righteous-

Righteousness is a gift

Alpha Series
Our True Identity

ness, as our own, if we are ever to have fellowship with God. How do we get it? How is this possible? The way we receive the righteousness of God, his gift, is said to be "by faith in Jesus Christ." This means you personally put *your* faith, and trust in what Jesus did for *you* when he died on the cross for *your* sins. You trust him to relate to you, not as just a member of the human race in some kind of corporate way, rather that he relates to you personally, individually through his death and resurrection.

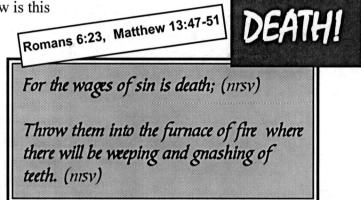

Romans 6:23, Matthew 13:47-51

DEATH!

For the wages of sin is death; (nrsv)

Throw them into the furnace of fire where there will be weeping and gnashing of teeth. (nrsv)

Rather than engage in some sort of self-improvement program we are called upon to simply believe in God's provisions for us in Christ. All who do so are said to be **"JUSTIFIED,"** —declared righteous by God, with his righteousness, because they trust him. Other biblical terms for this experience include being **"BORN AGAIN"**, **"SAVED"**, or **"REDEEMED"**. All sin must be paid for by someone (Romans 6:23). When Jesus laid down his righteous, eternal life, he paid the price one time for all sin, past, present, and future. *When you personally trust the fact that he died for you, you automatically, and without reservation or revocation, receive the righteousness of God.*

Figure 1, below, illustrates what takes place when we are born again. The outward triangle represents the personality structure that we received genetically from our parents. The plus and minus signs illustrate the positive and negative experiences that have shaped

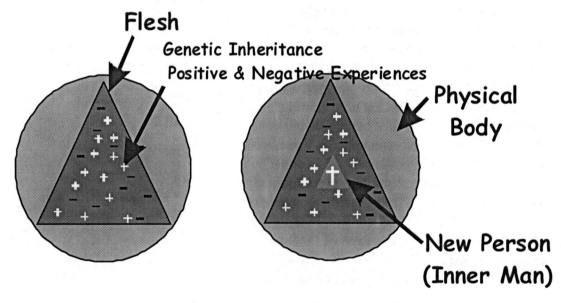

Alpha Series
Our True Identity

our personality content. As the "Old Man," (before we received Christ and his righteousness), we were naturally sinful and worthless. When we accept Jesus Christ as our personal Savior, however, God does a very miraculous thing by making us to be a brand new person, the "New Man," who has been given the righteousness of God. The smaller, white triangle on the inside represents the new person that has been born of the spirit, and shares the righteous character of God.

It is important to note the new person we are is still living in the same physical body, and is, therefore, still surrounded by the *natural conditioning* known biblically as *"the flesh"*. Figure 1 shows the brand new person surrounded by the "flesh" in the physical body. Generally speaking the Bible makes a distinction between the physical body, "flesh and blood", and the sinful nature, "the flesh", living within that body. While the physical body itself is essentially neutral, and can be used for good or evil, "the flesh", is the sinful nature or disposition toward sin, and may be viewed as the remnants of the old persons we were prior to the new birth. *It is the new man, (inward man), that has been born of God, and is, therefore, justified, (i.e. declared righteous by God).*

God's Regeneration Program

Since believers are really a brand new righteous person still living in a body that also houses a sinful nature, we are not surprised to find an intense inner conflict. It is to this inward turmoil of mixed motives, confused thoughts, and contradictory behavior that we now have to apply the gospel of Jesus Christ. The *total gospel* for believers is *more* than the fact that *we have been saved* from the guilt, and penalty of our sin. It also includes the fact that *we are now being saved* from the habit, dominion and power of sin in our lives. It is this gospel that Paul declares in Romans 6-8.

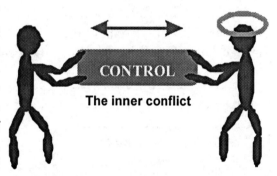

The inner conflict

The Flesh

- Sinful nature or disposition toward sin
- Natural pre-conditioning to trust in the world
- Human nature

What are we to do about our sin problem known as the "flesh"? Shall we just continue in sin that grace may abound? "God forbid!" Paul says, "How shall we, that are dead to sin live any longer therein?" (Romans 6:1,2). It is natural for baby Christians to become obsessed with their own or others sin, (dysfunction). They become

God's Regeneration Program

Alpha Series
Our True Identity

focused on trying to be good, not to sin and live the Christian life. But, Paul has a different focus for Christians. He shocks us into a new perspective on the problem of sin with this last question. Note carefully: *what he is really asking believers is this—how could they possibly go on sinning considering they are "dead to sin?"* Such a question shocks us at first. It implies, because we are "dead to sin," that we actually cannot go on sinning. In addition, the statement we are "dead to sin" shocks us because it is so foreign to our common experience of struggles against sin.

In the verses that follow, Paul clarifies this by revealing something that is wonderfully true about us as believers in Jesus Christ. He begins focusing our attention on *what God has already done about our sin problem* which produces both personal and relational dysfunction in our lives. He tells us that God has joined us to Christ, (baptized into Christ), in his death, burial and resurrection so that we may live a brand new life, (walk in newness of life). Elsewhere the bible assures us that this new life we receive is: (1) the life of Christ (Colossians 1:27, Galatians 2:20, Philippians 1:21); (2) lived by grace through faith (Col. 2:6, Gal. 2:21, 3:3, 5:16); and (3) directed by the mind of Christ (1 Cor. 2:9-16, Phil. 2:5-9, Rom. 12:2, Eph. 4:17-23).

> **The new life is:**
>
> The life of Christ
> (Colossians 1:27, Galatians 2:20, Philippians 1:21)
>
> Lived by grace through faith
> (Colossians 2:6, Galatians 2:21. 3:3, 5:16)
>
> Directed by the mind of Christ
> (1 Corinthians 2:9-16, Philippians 2:5-9, Romans 12:2, Ephesians 4:17-23)

> **Regardless of appearances**
>
> The Christian is dead to sin and Alive to God

To further explain the basis for our new life in Christ, Paul reveals that *the "old man", (i.e. the sinful, worthless person we were as natural descendants of Adam), is crucified once and for all*. The reasons God killed the "old man" that we were are given in the statements that follow. **First,** the old man is crucified so that "the body of sin might be destroyed". This means that our old man in Adam is legally pronounced dead in order that it should no longer condition or control the body. **Second,** the crucifixion of the old man frees us from the slavery to sin (habitual dysfunction) we naturally experienced all our lives. It is the crucifixion of the old man that makes us dead to sin "for he that is dead is freed from sin". **Finally,** the positive reason God crucified the old man (i.e. our sinful, worthless identity in Adam), is so that we could live in Christ. Because of our union with Christ we not only die with him, but we also live with him. God, being holy and righteous, cannot be joined to that which is unholy and unrighteous. He has put to death the old person we were, and raised up a new man that is holy and righteous so that we may live in

Alpha Series
Our True Identity

Christ.

In verse 11 we are called upon to apply the gospel in the preceding verses to our daily lives. We are commanded to "reckon (or count on the fact) that we are dead indeed to sin, but alive unto God through Jesus Christ our Lord". This requires the exercise of our faith to recognize and believe our true identity. God says he has changed our identity from being worthless in Adam to being worthy in Christ. As far as God is concerned, *we are already conformed to the image of Jesus Christ and, therefore, cannot continue in sin.* Our responsibility is not to "try hard not to sin," but rather to trust the fact that we are dead to sin, but alive unto God. *When we begin to focus our attention on who God has made us to be in Christ, we begin to experience the personal benefits of the gospel.* Only when we experience the security and significance we already have can we honestly be free of fear and confess our own "flesh" or sin nature to God. Such a confession underscores the divine forgiveness and cleansing we already have, and is necessary to mature as a child of God, and actually love others like Christ (1 John 1:9).

See the following page for a chart which depicts the qualities we enjoy in Christ.

> **Why the Old Man is dead**
>
> The Old Man is crucified and has no more control
>
> This crucifixion has set us free from the bondage of sin
>
> We have a new holy, perfect, and permanent identity in Christ

> **Where is your focus?**
>
> On living the Christian life?
> On trying to be good?
> Ensuring others are good?
> Going to church?
> Being religious?
> or
> On your true identity in Christ?

Alpha Series
Our True Identity

In Christ, We Are:

Loved	John 15:9; Rom. 5:5-8; 8:35-37; Eph. 2:4; 3:17-19
Accepted	Eph. 1:5-6; 2:13,19-22; Col. 1:22; Gal. 4:4-7; Rom. 8:14-17; 12:4,5; 1 Cor. 12:18-27
Forgiven	Rom. 8:1; Eph. 1:7; 2 Cor. 5:21; Col. 1:12-14; 2:13,14; 1 John 1:8-2:2
Important	John 15:5-8; 16; Eph. 2:10; 4:1-3, 11-16; Rom. 8:28,29; 1 Thes. 2:4; 5:14; Phil. 3:13,14
Adequate	1 Cor. 15:57,58; Eph. 3:20,21; 6:10; Phil. 1:6; 4:13
Needed	Rom. 15:1-7; John 13:34,35; 2 Cor. 1:3,4; Gal. 6:1,2;

Alpha Series
Our True Identity

QUESTIONS

CHAPTER FIVE: OUR TRUE IDENTITY

Lesson One: God's Regeneration Program

1. How do we change our false assumptions to the biblical assumption "I am worthy in Christ?"

2. What does Romans 3:10-18 say about the human nature apart from Christ?

3. What does Galatians 2:16 say about becoming righteous?

4. What is the purpose of the law?

5. What does Romans 3:21-28 say about how we are made righteous?

6. What happens to us when we are "born again," "justified," "saved," or "redeemed?"

7. What is Paul telling us in Romans 6:1-14? Focus on verse 11.

OUR TRUE IDENTITY — Chapter 5
THE PROMISE OF VICTORY — Lesson 2

Based upon the fact that we are joined to Christ in his death, burial and resurrection, all believers are commanded to count on the fact that they are dead indeed to sin and alive to God. To use other terms, *we are urged to change the false assumptions about ourselves to biblical assumptions concerning who we really are in Christ.* For example, we are to stop believing that we will be worthy, (more secure and significant), if we can make ourselves righteous; and start believing that God has

Romans 6:11

So you also must consider yourselves dead to sin and alive to God in Christ Jesus. (nrsv)

made us worthy already *by getting rid of the worthless person we were naturally, and raising us up in Christ as a brand new creation.* The unstated, and deadly motivation behind this "I will be worthy if ..." attitude is the belief

FAITH
Believing the unbelievable
Believing beyond our experiences
Believing beyond our circumstances
Believing beyond our pre-conditioning
Believing beyond our performance
Believing beyond our opinions
Believing beyond religion
Believing only God

Sin
Believing only the believable
Believing in our experiences
Believing in our circumstances
Believing in our pre-conditioning
Believing in our performance
Believing in our opinions
Believing in religion
Believing beyond God

"I am not worthy unless ..." This, of course, rejects all God has done for us, in Christ, that we could not do for ourselves. This attitude places our opinions and beliefs above what God says is true. This attitude says what God has done is incomplete, and needs something else —from me. It says I do not trust God! This attitude is sin.

God:

YOU ARE DEAD TO SIN,
ALIVE TO ME!
COUNT ON THIS WITH YOUR
WHOLE HEART!
COUNT ON THIS EVERY DAY!

Counting on the fact that we are dead to sin (the attitude of counting on anything else but God), and alive to God (counting on him alone) is the central issue of faith that all Christians must contend with on a daily basis. The Bible assures us that the just, (those who are born again), shall *keep on living by faith,* and that without faith it is impossible to please God. What God wants from us is not another empty promise to behave our-

Alpha Series
Our True Identity

selves, but our faith in what he has done to make us worthy. Such faith, as we shall see in later studies, will put us into a completely different life-style that blesses God, and loves others.

> **Two distinct life-styles**
> Receiving the gospel - grace
> Rejecting the gospel - law

In Romans 6:12-14 the apostle Paul outlines two distinct life-styles that we may live in depending on whether or not we exercise the faith called for in counting ourselves dead to sin, and alive unto God. In receiving the gospel of what God has done about our sin problem we may enter into a new life-style that is functional and healthy. In rejecting the gospel of our new identity in Christ we remain locked into the old dysfunctional life-style.

To understand the initial command to not allow sin to reign in our mortal bodies, it is necessary to define what we mean by sin. The term "sin" in the singular needs to be distinguished from "sins" in the plural. The singular refers to the nature of sin which we shall call unbelief, while the plural has to do with specific acts of transgressing God's law. When Paul tells us to stop allowing sin to reign, he is not telling us to simply quit doing acts that are wrong, but rather to *stop allowing unbelief to dominate our lives.*

> **Understanding sin**
> Sins: Specific acts of transgression
> Sin: The attitude of unbelief

Allowing sin to reign is neither a behavior nor a feeling, but *a mental attitude composed of certain beliefs that have been developed by past experiences.* From birth to rebirth we were dominated by the "Old Man" and his depraved nature as described earlier. We were born spiritually dead, and until we came to salvation we were "dead in trespasses and sins", we "walked according to the course of this world," and were 'fulfilling the desires of the flesh" (Ephesians 2:1-3). All of our experiences were associated with the reign of the "Old Man." We believed, we knew, we were certain, we were doomed to sin and failure.

> **Romans 14:23**
> *... because they do not act from faith; for whatever does not proceed from faith is sin. (nrsv)*

In spite of our best efforts to find personal worth in the things, relationships and activities of this world, we still experienced a gnawing sense of emptiness and worthlessness. *We were conditioned to believe that*

> **Allowing sin to reign**
> Allowing sin to reign is neither a behavior nor a feeling, but a mental attitude composed of certain beliefs that have been developed by past experiences.

> Where is the peace and joy?

84   **The Promise of Victory**

Alpha Series
Our True Identity

the best we could hope for was the temporary pleasures of the natural life.

At the moment we received Jesus Christ as our personal savior, we experienced something totally new and different in our lives. For the first time we knew the joy and satisfaction of true personal worth. As we received forgiveness, and the Holy Spirit assured us of our acceptance by God as adopted children, we experienced a sense of relief, comfort and peace all mixed together. Because we believed that Jesus paid for our sins on the cross, we were saved from the *guilt and penalty* of sin, and enjoyed a new perspective on ourselves, God, and life itself.

But, what happened to our new-found joy and satisfaction? Why is it that so many of us seem to fade back into the same old quality of life we had before salvation? The answer most often given to these questions usually implies that our loss of joy and satisfaction is somehow due to our conduct as a Christian.

> **Ephesians 2:1-3**
>
> ¹ *In the past you were spiritually dead because of your sins and the things you did against God.* ² *Yes, in the past you lived the way the world lives, following the ruler of the evil powers that are above the earth. That same spirit is now working in those who refuse to obey God.* ³ *In the past all of us lived like them, trying to please our sinful selves and doing all the things our bodies and minds wanted. We should have suffered God's anger because of the way we were. We were the same as all other people.* (ncv)

> False repentance?
> or
> True repentance?

The danger with this answer is that it implies our joy and satisfaction will be restored only if we do the right things. Joy and peace never come from our performance, they always come from the inside out. If we experience any joy and peace, based upon our conduct, our focus is incorrect, and we are misled. Peace and joy come from faith, hope and love.

Accepting this sort of answer, however, many of us have determined to change our conduct in some way. We might try *more Bible study, more worship, more witnessing, more giving, etc.*, only to discover sometime later that *we still lack the joy we once knew*. Spurred on by an emotional appeal from the pulpit, or an inspirational praise service, we may try another flurry of good works, and still fail to find true satisfaction. Finally, we may become so frustrated that we resign ourselves to the false belief that the Christian life is simply a dreary set of obligations with little or no reward in this

> **Beliefs resulting from false repentance**
>
> We were never really saved
> or
> We shall always experience an empty defeated life.

The Promise of Victory

life. Once again, our thinking has been conditioned by our experiences, rather than what God says. We have not *truly* repented because we do not know the truth.

The key to maintaining or regaining the joy of our salvation is obviously not in *changing our behavior (false repentance)*, but in *changing our beliefs (true repentance)*. The loss of joy as a Christian is associated with the realization that we yet possess a sinful nature left behind by the "Old Man." Many Christians are shocked to discover that they still have the same old sinful desires that they had before they were saved. An even greater shock is experienced when we find ourselves doing the one thing we thought we would never do again. We begin to think of ourselves as being the "Old Man" again, and may even try to **control ourselves** with a set of **rules and regulations** rather than *faith in what God has done for us*. The harder we try to behave the more *we concentrate on our failures and sin*. The more obsessed we become with our sin the more we are likely to fail again. Finally, we conclude that (1) we were never really saved, or (2) we shall always experience an empty defeated life. We have never experienced true repentance! Rather, we are still counting on the old ways of false repentance concerned with behavior modification.

It is at this point that Paul's instruction in Romans 6:11 must be believed, and the command of Romans 6:12, understood and obeyed. Under grace, obedience is always understood to be "walking by faith." Rather than being shocked and dominated by evidence of our sinful nature, *we are to exercise faith, and count on the fact that we are dead to sin, that the real person we are does not sin. We are to "walk by faith."* The reign of sin in our mortal body is broken by faith in the fact that we are truly dead to sin but alive unto God. *We are new creatures who cannot sin!* Believing in who God has made us to be in Christ is the only way we can ever cope with the habit and dominion of sin in our lives.

Alternative Life-styles

There are two alternative life-styles presented in verses 12 and 13 of Romans 6. Which one applies to you is determined by what you choose to believe. The first, the life-style of grace, is lived by counting on the fact that we are *dead to sin, and alive unto God*. This basic faith concerning our union with Christ gives us the healthy and true self-image we need to have personal hope. *Hope* is that joyful and confident expectation about our future which *tells us that all is well*. From that hope comes the ability to consider the needs of others, and actually love them like Christ.

The second life-style, the life-style of law, is based on natural unbelief that says we are *alive unto sin, and dead to God*. This is how most people, especially Christians, view themselves. This assumption is based upon viewing our performance as the basis of being alive to God. The lack of faith concerning our being one with Christ gives us the dysfunctional self-image of being worthless. Thinking of ourselves as being sinful and

Alpha Series
Our True Identity

The alternative beliefs:

1. You are dead to sin and alive to God (Grace)
   or
2. You are dead to God and alive to sin (Law)

worthless we are driven by the "lusts of the flesh" to make ourselves feel worthy at any cost. Rather than love and minister to others we will naturally hate and manipulate.

Figure 1 summarizes the two life-styles presented in these verses with regard to our thoughts, emotions, and behavior.

We may either believe what God says he has made us to be, and be free, or reject it, and remain in fear of failure, in fear of rejection, and in bondage to sin. If we believe who we are in Christ we will experience the hope necessary to 'yield ourselves to God as those who are alive from the dead," and be used by God as his instrument to love others. Other-

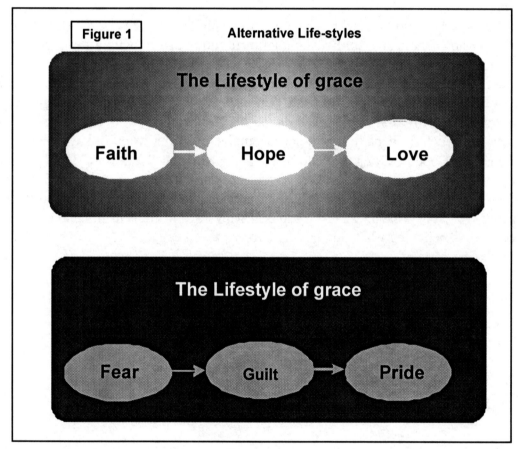

wise, our fears will drive us to cope with life in the typical dysfunctional ways.

In telling us to count ourselves dead to sin, and alive unto God, Paul assures us, with a final explanation, *sin shall never again have dominion over us, the real us.* We died with Christ on the cross, and our "Old Man" has been put to death, and a new man has been

The Promise of Victory

Alpha Series
Our True Identity

raised up. The "New Man" is that new person God made us to be "in Christ." That "New Man" is a brand new identity (name) we receive. *We are inseparably joined to Christ, and we shall never again be dominated by sin.* As far as God is concerned, we

> **Your identity**
> You are not a sinner (Old Man) saved by grace,
> You are a saint (New Man) born by grace.

are the "New Man," and as such, we are eternally separated from the sin nature known as our flesh. That sin will not have dominion over us does not imply the sin nature or flesh is eradicated or ceases to exist. It simply means that God has made an eternal distinction between who we now are in Christ and our leftover fleshly nature. *He has separated the sin from the sinner by putting to death the old person we were, and raising up a brand new person.*

Although the "Old Person" has been put to death, the "New Person," who we have become (who cannot sin), still lives in a leftover "body of sin" with a flesh nature that never quits sinning. In the next few chapters we will consider, in detail, what is necessary to overcome the flesh, the leftover sin nature. Faith is needed. We must first learn to trust that God has separated us from our flesh. **Our faith in what God has done to separate us from our flesh is the first step in overcoming the flesh.**

Our separation from the flesh was not accomplished by our works of law-keeping, but by the grace of God in killing the "Old Man," and raising the "New Man." *Paul explains that sin will not have the ultimate victory over us because we are not under law but grace.* The law can only demand a righteous life, and condemn to death those who fail to meet its demands. The only possible way for us to deal with sin, and all its dysfunction, is by the grace of God, believing what God has done for you, you cannot do for yourself. This is living the life-style of grace.

Alpha Series
Our True Identity

QUESTIONS

CHAPTER FIVE: OUR TRUE IDENTITY

Lesson Two: The Promise of Victory

1. What is it we are supposed to count on every day?

2. What are the two distinct life-styles Paul refers to in Romans 6:12-14?

3. What is the difference between the singular use of the term sin and the plural use?

4. In this case then, to what is Paul referring in verse 12 when he tells us not to let sin reign in our lives?

5. What are some of the ways we try to be good and change our own behavior?

6. Relate this behavior to the Solomon syndrome and the idea of false goals and false assumptions.

7. What terms are used to describe the life-styles of law and grace?

8. In overcoming the flesh, what is the first step?

Alpha Series
Our True Identity

THE MIRROR — Chapter 6
THE OLD AND NEW COVENANTS — Lesson 1

The promise that sin shall not have dominion over us is good news for all who are struggling with personal and relational problems. Since the root of all our problems may be traced back to unbelief concerning our personal worth (false assumptions) the promise that we may be set free from the sin of unbelief offers tremendous hope to all who will receive it by faith.

In the last chapter we began to study the biblical basis for our worth as persons so that we might know the truth that sets us free. *Our attention has been turned away from our own efforts to save ourselves, and directed toward what God says He's doing about our sin problem.* We learned that God has joined us to Christ in his death, burial, and resurrection in order to put to death the sinful person we were and raise up a brand new person to live out a new life in Christ. *Our responsibility is to simply believe what God said he has done for us in spite of the evidence to the contrary.* When we do so, we enter into a healthy lifestyle of grace and truth that assures us sin will not have dominion over us.

> Joined to Christ
> Set free
> Old Man put to death
> New Man is raised
> Believe... despite circumstances and experience

In this study we will explore more fully how we are changed by the lifestyle of grace by contrasting it with the natural lifestyle of law. This contrast is not simply a matter of religious preference or a subject of theological debate. It is ultimately a contrast between freedom and bondage, and life and death.

The Old and New Covenants

In his second letter to the Corinthian church, Paul encourages believers to fulfill their purpose in life as servants of Christ or "ministers" of Christ's love for others. In the third chapter he tells us that "our sufficiency is of God" (2 Corinthians 3:5), meaning all we are, and all we do, is ultimately from God. Paul says our worth, as persons, is based entirely upon what God has done for us in Christ that we could not do for ourselves. He further instructs us that we *are* "able ministers" or adequate servants of the "New Testament," (as opposed to the Old Testament or covenant) and begins drawing a contrast between the two covenants of law and grace.

To grasp the significance of this contrast requires that we know what Paul means by the terms "New and Old Covenants." The King James translation uses the

> Our sufficiency is of God, Able ministers

term "testament" which is synonymous with the term "covenant," and literally means a contract. In this contrast between the New Covenant and the Old Covenant we are going to contrast two kinds of contracts God has made with man. The New Covenant is a contract of grace, whereas the Old Covenant is a contract of law. Thus, the contrast Paul is revealing in this chapter is really the difference between law and grace, and their respective life-styles.

Covenant = contract
Testament

The Old Covenant of law was established when God gave the ten commandments to Moses at Mount Sinai. The terms of that contract were essentially a promise of blessing for obedience to all of God's commands, and a promise of cursing for transgressing those commands. In short God said, "If you keep my commandments I will bless you, but if you disobey them I will curse you." This is the same kind of covenant that God made with Adam and Eve concerning the tree of the knowledge of good and evil in the Garden of Eden. **In the Garden, as under**

The Old Covenant
Conditional
Performance based
Blessings for obedience
Curses for disobedience

The New Covenant
Unconditional
Grace based
An intimate personal relationship with God is provided

Jeremiah 31:31-34

> *31 "Look, the time is coming, says the LORD, when I will make a new agreement with the people of Israel and the people of Judah.*
> *32 It will not be like the agreement I made with their ancestors when I took them by the hand to bring them out of Egypt. I was a husband to them, but they broke that agreement, says the LORD.*
> *33 This is the agreement I will make with the people of Israel at that time, says the LORD: I will put my teachings in their minds and write them on their hearts. I will be their God, and they will be my people.*
> *34 People will no longer have to teach their neighbors and relatives to know the LORD, because all people will know me, from the least to the most important, says the LORD. I will forgive them for the wicked things they did, and I will not remember their sins anymore.* (ncv)

Sinai, the blessings of God had to be earned and maintained by the obedience of man.

In contrast to the Old Covenant of law, the New Covenant of grace is unconditional rather than conditional in nature. By this we mean that God's blessings are not conditioned upon man's obedience or efforts of any sort. In Jeremiah 31:31-34 the prophet announces the terms of the new covenant that outline God's unconditional blessings in grace. First, God said, *"...I will put my law in their inward parts, and write it in their hearts..."* (verse 33). This is a promise that God would give us the inward motivation, and knowledge necessary to do His will. Second, He said, *"...they shall all know me, from the least of them to the greatest of them..."* (verse 34). This refers to the ability for all to have an intimate, personal relationship with God. Finally, he states, *"...I will forgive their iniquity, and remember their sin no more."* (verse 34). God will provide total forgiveness of sins and deliver us forever from condemnation.

The Letter Kills, The Spirit Gives Life

The life and death contrast between the lifestyles of law and grace is demonstrated by the effect each has on the believer. Paul uses the term "letter" to refer to the lifestyle under the Old Covenant of law. In so doing he emphasizes the object of faith under a law system, which is the "letter of the law." By the term, "letter" Paul is referring to our own interpretation of the law as it applies to certain situations, often making it fit situations it should not. For instance, the law said to remember the Sabbath to keep it holy. The Pharisee's "letter" (interpretation) concerning that particular law was —Jesus should not heal people on the sabbath!

By contrasting the letter of the law with the Spirit of grace, Paul shows us our faith should be placed in the *personal* leadership of the Holy Spirit rather than *our* interpretation of the law.

> *Living the Christian life by your efforts is living by the letter of the law.*

> *Trying to be a good Christian is living by the letter of the law*

Living under the law demands that we lean on our own understanding and rely upon our own knowledge of good and evil to guide our every step. Besides causing us personal frustration or spiritual pride, *relying upon the letter of the law simply does not work to produce a righteous life.* It is the personal leadership and power of the indwelling Holy Spirit we must learn to trust. In Galatians chapter 3, Paul rebuked those Christians who try to live the Christian life in the natural energy of the religious flesh rather than rely upon the leadership and power of the Holy Spirit.

A good example of this contrast between the Spirit and the letter, may be found in the subject of the tithe. The law of the tithe given to us in Deuteronomy 14:22-26 is radically different from the typical interpretation or "letter" of the tithe today. Typically, we think

Alpha Series
The Mirror

> **The law brings death**
> **The Spirit brings life**

of tithing as simply giving ten percent of our money to the church or some sort of ministry. The original law of the tithe in Deuteronomy, however, suggests that part, if not all of the tithe was to be spent "for whatever thy soul desireth," (Deut. 14:26). There are many preachers today who would, no doubt, interpret this passage in a variety of ways, and offer us a "letter" of the law we could trust. It would be far better to simply ask the Holy Spirit, living within, to lead us in our giving instead of reviewing the various interpretations of the law of the tithe.

> **The only way not to live by the letter of the law is to live being led by the Spirit of God**

The result of listening to the Holy Spirit in this giving issue, or any other issue, will be "life" as opposed to that of following the letter which is "death". *The function of the law is to show how desperately we need a savior.* It does this by demanding absolute perfection, and condemning to death those who fail to meet its demands. Thus, Paul says, "the letter kills."

> **The Spirit**
> Convicts us of sin
> Gives us faith

> **The law**
> The law shows us how desperately we need a savior

The Spirit, however, not only reveals sin to us, *but also gives us the faith* we need to trust in Jesus. In addition, the Spirit regenerates, indwells, seals, fills and baptizes us into Christ. It is the Holy Spirit who also fills or controls us, empowers, leads, teaches, reminds and comforts us. Thus the "Spirit gives life" in the fullest sense.

From Glory to Glory

The remaining verses of 2 Corinthians chapter 3, complete the contrast between law and grace in terms of glory. The word, "glory", has many uses ranging from a state of blissful joy to simply a public display of character. Here the contrast between law and grace is viewed as the difference between glory and more glory, in its fullest meaning.

Under the law there is a certain glory in keeping the commands of God, and pointing out how others have failed. One of the most natural ways of making ourselves look good is to make others look bad, or put others down. The law can be used to make us look good when we do manage to live up to certain standards while others fail. In addition to this hypocritical glory, the law, given by God at Mount Sinai, was a truly glorious event. God publicly displayed His righteous character on the mount, in the written law, and through the shining face of Moses.

Glorious as this occasion was, however, Paul says that the glory of this "ministry of

Alpha Series
The Mirror

death" (the giving of the law) is far surpassed by the glory of the "ministry of the Spirit" (the giving of life capable of producing in us the righteousness demanded by the law). It is one thing to demand that people behave themselves, it's quite another to make them behave. The law has a certain glory in it as it demands righteousness, and condemns the unrighteous; but the Spirit of grace is far more glorious in that *the indwelling Spirit actually produces the righteousness* demanded by the law.

The practical application of this contrast between law and grace is summarized in the last verse of the chapter. Unlike the hypocrisy of Moses who kept a veil over his face so the people couldn't see that his face wasn't shining anymore, Paul says we can be honest, transparent and real in our relationships when we live in grace rather than under the law. With "open" or unveiled faces, (being honest with ourselves and God), we may steadfastly look into the mirror of God's word to see who we are in Christ. This is exactly what we are doing at this point in our study, i.e. looking at Romans 6, 7 and 8 to see who we are in Christ, the glory of the Lord.

When we see who we are in Christ, revealed by the illumination of the Holy Spirit in our minds, we are changed into the same image from glory to glory. Note that he does not say we look into the mirror, the Bible, to see what changes need to be made, and then try hard to change ourselves.

> The ministry of the Spirit Surpasses the glory of the law

That's the "letter" again, and it will not work. Instead, he says that we look into the Bible to see who we are in Christ, (the glory of the Lord), and a miracle takes place as we are changed into the same image by the personal work of the Spirit within. This change is "from glory to glory" which means it is developmental in nature and will continue to take place throughout our lives. But this change is done by the Spirit of God, and not ourselves. Thus, living in the grace of God by the Spirit is the only functional life we may experience; all else is death.

Alpha Series
The Mirror

QUESTIONS

CHAPTER SIX: THE MIRROR

Lesson One: The Old and New Covenants

1. What is a covenant?

2. What is the difference between the Old Covenant and the New Covenant, in the way we live out our lives?

3. What does Paul mean by the "letter of the law?"

4. What is the purpose of the law? Has that been accomplished in you?

5. What is the contrast Paul draws between the "glory of the ministry of death (living by law)" and the "glory of the ministry of the Spirit (living by faith)?"

THE MIRROR
SLAVES TO RIGHTEOUSNESS

Chapter 6 — Lesson 2

The good news that sin shall not have dominion over us because we are not under law, but under grace, (Romans 6:14), is almost to good to be true. In our natural minds we have trouble accepting the terms of the new covenant of grace. They go against our conditioning of so many years, of so many experiences, and so many circumstances. Based upon this conditioning, we have been trying very hard to earn the approval and blessings of others by our own efforts. Now, comes the Word of God, reversing all our conditioning by telling us to believe that it is *God* who causes us to keep His law; that *He will* enjoy an intimate and personal relationship with us; that *He will* forget all our sins. This is so foreign to our carnal (natural) minds we naturally confuse God's grace with a license to sin.

> **Jeremiah 31:33-34**
>
> ³³ *"This is the agreement I will make with the people of Israel at that time," says the LORD: "I will put my teachings in their minds and write them on their hearts. I will be their God, and they will be my people."*
> ³⁴ *"People will no longer have to teach their neighbors and relatives to know the LORD, because all people will know me, from the least to the most important," says the LORD. "I will forgive them for the wicked things they did, and I will not remember their sins anymore."* (ncv)

In the closing verses of Romans 6, the apostle Paul raises the question of perverting God's grace in the new covenant. "What then? Shall we sin, because we are not under the law, but under grace? God forbid!" (Romans 6:15) No doubt Paul encountered this question constantly as he tried to teach the new lifestyle of grace to those who were steeped in legalism, as we all are. One of the first questions to arise in the natural, legal mentality would have been something along this line..." since we aren't under the law are we free to sin?" *Because of the radical nature of the gospel of grace, the natural mind would see it as an open invitation to sin all the more without any fear of the consequences.*

> **Romans 6:15**
>
> **Perversion of the gospel**
>
> *What then? Shall we sin, because we are not under the law, but under grace? God forbid!* (nrsv)

Alpha Series
The Mirror

The perversion of the Gospel

Ignores:

We are free from the dominion of sin as well as the penalty of sin.

The Old Man has been put to death

The New Man has been raised

Our being new creations

The Holy Spirit who lives within us.

We have new motivations

A shallow understanding of the lifestyle of grace sees only the fact that God has freed us from the penalty of sin under the law. It ignores altogether the fact that we are free so we may *now* enjoy the blessings of living a supernatural life which is free from the *dominion* of sin as well as the penalty of sin. It ignores altogether our being new creations with new motivations generated by God through the work of the Holy Spirit who lives within us. Such an idea

The life-style of grace

Is composed of two elements:

1. Freedom from the penalty of sin and
2. Freedom from the power of sin

does not understand the gospel of grace which puts to death the "Old Man," and raises a "New Man." Such thinking forgets the "new birth." *The grace of God by which we are delivered from **both the penalty and power of sin** is perverted by the selfish notion that our freedom from the penalty of sin is a license to go on sinning.*

The *lifestyle* of grace is fully understood as a special privilege of yielding ourselves to God, through his Spirit, to love others just like Christ. The lifestyle of grace is not to be understood as only freedom from the penalty of sin under the law. When the lifestyle of grace is fully understood, the only appropriate answer to this question of license to sin is Paul's statement, "God forbid," or "may it never be!"

Servants of Righteousness or Sin?

To explain his short answer, "God forbid", Paul goes on to first describe a fundamental principle of obedience. He states that we are the servants to whomever we choose to yield ourselves (that is we become slaves according to whom we choose to serve) whether it be to sin which leads to death, or obedience to God which leads to righteousness. *There is no middle ground when it comes to dedication, or yielding ourselves. The two, sin and God, are opposed to each other.* In choosing not to yield ourselves to God, we dedicate ourselves to sin. In choosing to dedicate ourselves to God, we

Alpha Series
The Mirror

Galatians 5:16-18

> 16 "So I tell you: Live by following the Spirit. Then you will not do what your sinful selves want.
> 17 Our sinful selves want what is against the Spirit, and the Spirit wants what is against our sinful selves. The two are against each other, so you cannot do just what you please.
> 18 But if the Spirit is leading you, you are not under the law." (ncv)

cannot possibly serve sin, (Galatians 5:16-18).

Based on this principle Paul reminds us that we are all slaves to God. Whereas we were at one time the slaves to sin (Eph. 2:1-3), God is to be thanked for His grace whereby we "obeyed *from the heart* that form of doctrine" unto which we were made committed (emphasis added, Eph. 2:4-10). By this statement Paul means that God is to be thanked for the grace of committing us to the gospel message that we might obey it by a response of faith from the heart. This obedience of faith *from the heart* is all of God, not self-generated. On the basis of the God-given ability to obey from the heart, we were made slaves to the gospel message of deliverance from the power as well as the penalty of sin.

The thought is continued in verses 17 and 18, which tell us that when we were set free from our natural slavery to sin, we became a slave to righteousness. Taken together, the two verses present a beautiful description of salvation not only from the penalty, but *also from the power of sin*. Thus, the idea of continuing in sin because we are not under law is absolutely absurd! The lifestyle of grace means we are slaves to righteousness rather than sin. An "about face" has occurred; a renewing of the mind; repentance. Paul is quick to add that he is speaking "after the manner of men" in that he draws an analogy between the obedience of a slave to his master, and the obedience of a believer to God. What he has just described in

A fundamental principle of obedience

We are the servants to whomever we choose to yield ourselves

The keys to the lifestyle of grace

➤ Remember your true identity
➤ Count on the fact that we are dead to sin and alive unto God
➤ Count on the fact that we have been made slaves to righteousness

terms of slavery is actually the highest form of freedom we can ever know. Man was once compelled to follow human nature (without freedom to do otherwise), but now has been set free. This freedom to serve the God of the universe is the greatest liberty man can ever experience. We are set "free indeed" from bondage to the human sin nature; we are delivered from the power of sin.

Verse 19 concludes with an appeal for

Slaves to Righteousness

us to exercise our responsibility in realizing our new identity in Christ by faith; the key to the lifestyle of grace. Just as he has called on us to count on the fact that we are dead to sin, and alive unto God, (Romans 6:11), *we are also to count on the fact that we have been made slaves to righteousness*. The only thing that can keep us from sinning because we are no longer under the law is the new identity that we have in Christ as a slave to righteousness. Although it is ultimately God himself that made us slaves to righteousness, our responsibility, as always, is to believe who God has made us to be. When we believe we are now slaves to righteousness we can yield our "members servants to righteousness unto holiness." Again the key to living in the grace of God is a matter of faith in who God has made us to be. We are not only "dead indeed unto sin", but we are miraculously "alive unto God". Believing that God has made us slaves to righteousness is necessary for us to yield ourselves to his service.

> **Appeal for responsibility** — **Romans 6:19**
>
> *I use this example because this is hard for you to understand. In the past you offered the parts of your body to be slaves to sin and evil; you lived only for evil. In the same way now you must give yourselves to be slaves of goodness. Then you will live only for God.* (ncv)

Eternal Life Through Jesus

In the closing verses of the chapter, Paul contrasts the result of being a slave to sin to the result of being a slave to righteousness. The question, "What fruit had ye...", is designed to point out that being a slave to sin has it's fruit: the emptiness, shame, and the personal death of a dysfunctional lifestyle; while on the other hand, being a slave to righteousness, yields "fruit unto holiness, and the end everlasting life." The life that is motivated by faith in our new identity in Christ is not empty or dysfunctional. Instead, it produces fruit that is characterized by holiness (i.e. the fruit of the Spirit—Gal. 5:22,23), and will lead us into true personal and spiritual life.

It is important to note the difference in the terms used for each type of service. For the service to sin, the results are referred to as "wages". This means we received all we earned by our natural human efforts under a law system. *"Wages" always refers to what must be earned.* In contrast, the results of our service to righteousness are referred to as a "gift of God". *"Gift" always refers to what cannot be earned.* This suggests that *both the service itself, and the results* of that service are gifts of God. **We do not serve God to earn or keep our eternal life; in fact, it is impossible to do so.** On the contrary, God has *freely* given us His eternal life. Based upon that gift we are *made* slaves to righteousness, and are able to serve Him out of a pure heart of love and gratitude. And even this pure heart of

Alpha Series
The Mirror

love and gratitude is a gift from God. We cannot have it by human effort. The law says, "Do this, and live." Grace says "Live, and do this."

From a divine point of view we cannot go on sinning because God has made us slaves to righteousness. From a human point of view we no longer want to continue in sin because God's grace has made us brand new persons who are raised up to walk in newness of a functional, healthy lifestyle the Bible calls "eternal life". More will be said about how we live this new lifestyle in the grace of God in later chapters. For now, it is enough to know that living in grace is not a license to go on sinning, rather, the only way we can possibly quit sinning.

> **Fruit of the Spirit** — Galatians 5:22-25
>
> *22 By contrast, the fruit of the Spirit is love, joy, peace, patience, kindness, generosity, faithfulness,"*
> *23 "gentleness, and self-control. There is no law against such things."*
> *24 "And those who belong to Christ Jesus have crucified the flesh with its passions and desires."*
> *25 "If we live by the Spirit, let us also be guided by the Spirit." (nrsv)*

As we look into the mirror of God's word to see the real persons we are, we discover that God has joined us to Christ, making us truly dead indeed to sin. It is, therefore, impossible for *the real persons we are* "to continue in sin that grace may abound." It is just as impossible to go on sinning because we are not under law, but under grace. Having been made slaves to righteousness, it is ridiculous for us to do anything but yield ourselves to God.

> **Terms for service**
>
> Wages always refers to what must be earned
>
> Gift always refers to what cannot be earned

Remembering who we are we live as children of the King not as children of the gutter. We live by yielding ourselves "as those that are alive from the dead." meaning we are believing we both died and rose again in Christ. We live yielding "our members servants to righteousness unto holiness." Although the flesh still surrounds the new persons we are and wars against every attempt to live like Christ; and even though the flesh may show itself, we are assured we are not our flesh. Our daily task as believers is, first, and foremost, to believe we are no longer our flesh, yield ourselves unto God, and our members as slaves to righteousness.

> Law: Do this and live
>
> Grace: Live and do this

Slaves to Righteousness

Alpha Series
The Mirror

QUESTIONS

CHAPTER SIX: THE MIRROR

Lesson two: Slaves to righteousness.

1. Who is it that causes us to keep the law?

2. What perversion of the gospel does Paul address in Romans 6:15?

3. What does the perversion or misunderstanding of grace imply about understanding the New Covenant?

4. What is a fundamental principle of obedience?

5. What are the keys to the lifestyle of grace?

6. What are the two terms designated as service and what is the difference?

WHO SHALL DELIVER ME?
Chapter 7
DEAD TO THE LAW — Lesson 1

The promise that sin (with all its dysfunction) shall not have dominion over us is based upon the fact that we are no longer under the law, but under grace. Having considered and dealt with the natural tendency to pervert this great promise into a license to sin, *Paul goes on to explain the basis of this promise as our death to the law.* By grace through our faith in the gospel message the old, sinful, dysfunctional person we were by nature was crucified, and buried with Christ, and a new person was raised up with Christ to be a servant of righteousness. To the extent that we accept this new identity by faith we are progressively changed into the image of Christ. To continue to live, and grow in the grace of God requires that we understand what it means to be *dead, not only to sin, but also to the law.*

The Dominion of the Law

In the first three verses of Romans 7, Paul uses an analogy from marriage to illustrate the law has dominion over a man as long as he lives. Just as a married woman is bound to her husband by law as long as the husband lives, so also the natural man is under the bondage and condemnation of the law as long as he lives his natural life as the "Old Man." But if the woman's husband dies, she is free to marry another. Death is required to break the dominion of the law. As long as we live the natural life we were born with as the "Old Man," we are under the demands and condemnation of the law.

> **Types of law**
> Parental
> Social
> Peer
> Civil
> Religious
> God's

> *Death is required to break the dominion of the law*

But what is meant by the law? Exactly what are we dead to? The following explains what Paul meant when he said, "we know the law".

Parental law

We were first introduced to "the law" by our parents or guardians who raised us as children. We were told what to do, when to do it, when not to do it, where to go, how to act, etc. Our lives were strictly regimented by an external set of rules and regulations that, for the most part, were meant to protect us.

Alpha Series
Who Shall Deliver Me?

Social law
When we went to school we were introduced to a "social law" system as we begin to learn how to behave outside our own home, and relate to others. The socialization process involved learning what is and what is not allowed in the society we grew up in so that we would hopefully become productive members someday.

Peer law
About that same time, however, we also began to be shaped by yet another law system given to us by our peers. Their rules and regulations had to be obeyed in order for us to fit in with that particular group. While the law system of our peers may have been radically different from that of our parents or teachers, (i.e. gang rules), it was law nonetheless.

Civil law
As we grow up, and become aware of the community around us we began to also be aware of the laws that govern our communities, states, and nation. The civil law systems ranging from city ordinances to state statutes and federal laws are meant to govern the society we live in, and are necessary to preserve it.

Religious law
When we go to church we encounter yet another law system of rules and regulations. Religious law varies from church to church, and may either be expressed in written or unwritten forms. The particular rules of a religious system will generally concern conduct within the home and community as well as the church itself. Virtually all important events in life will be addressed by religious law in some fashion.

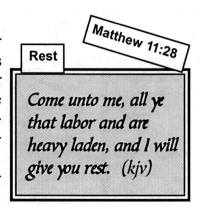

Rest — Matthew 11:28
Come unto me, all ye that labor and are heavy laden, and I will give you rest. (kjv)

God's law
Finally our exposure to the dominion of the law also includes God's law as revealed in the Bible. Beginning with the ten commandments in the Old Testament, we discover that God has revealed very specific laws that address all areas of our lives. As far as the law is concerned, the New Testament scriptures are much more intense in that there are over 1,000 commands which require, for the most part, supernatural ability to obey.

Alpha Series
Who Shall Deliver Me?

Each one of these law systems carry with them certain demands and expectations that we have been trying to live up to all our lives. Such a heavy burden is what Paul refers to as the dominion of the law that keeps us in personal bondage. Jesus offered us freedom in His great invitation in Matthew 11:28, when he said, "Come unto me, all ye that labor, and are heavy laden, and I will give you rest."

The Believer's Death to the Law

Applying the analogy of the married woman to our own situation we are assured in verse four that all believers have been made "dead to the law by the body of Christ". The way this happens is described earlier in chapter six as the death of the "Old Man," and the creation of the "New Man." (Romans 6:6-10). The natural person we were was put to death, and a new person was raised up. The death of the "Old Man," which separates us from the law, is analogous to the death of the woman's husband, which legally separates and frees her from her husband, the law.

As noted earlier, we are all naturally "married" to the law of our parents, society, peers, religion, etc. When the old person we were was crucified with Christ, our bondage to the law was broken so that the new person is now free to be "married" (i.e. joined), to Christ. (Our freedom from the "Old Man," and the law which dominated that "Old Man" is said to be accomplished in the death of Christ on the cross, (see also Colossians 2:10-14)).

The necessity for our becoming dead to the law is implied in the latter part of verse 7:4 of Romans. *There, we are given the purpose of our death to the law: "that ye should be married to another. (kjv)"* Why? *"That we should bring forth fruit unto God. (kjv)"* As was pointed out in an earlier study, it is absolutely impossible for anyone to live up to the righteous demands of God's law in his own strength. While we may meet some of the expectations of our parent's law, or stay within the boundaries of civil, or even religious law, *we can never meet the demands of God's law for absolute perfection by ourselves.*

Romans 6:6-10 — **Dead to the law**

⁶ *We know that our old self was crucified with him so that the body of sin might be destroyed, and we might no longer be enslaved to sin."*
⁷ *For whoever has died is freed from sin."*
⁸ *But if we have died with Christ, we believe that we will also live with him."*
⁹ *We know that Christ, being raised from the dead, will never die again; death no longer has dominion over him."*
¹⁰ *The death he died, he died to sin, once for all; but the life he lives, he lives to God. (nrsv)*

Alpha Series
Who Shall Deliver Me?

Raised to new life — **Colossians 2:10-14**

¹⁰ and you have a full and true life in Christ, who is ruler over all rulers and powers." ¹¹ Also in Christ you had a different kind of circumcision, a circumcision not done by hands. It was through Christ's circumcision, that is, his death, that you were made free from the power of your sinful self." ¹² When you were baptized, you were buried with Christ, and you were raised up with him through your faith in God's power that was shown when he raised Christ from the dead." ¹³ When you were spiritually dead because of your sins and because you were not free from the power of your sinful self, God made you alive with Christ, and he forgave all our sins." ¹⁴ He canceled the debt, which listed all the rules we failed to follow. He took away that record with its rules and nailed it to the cross. (ncv)

Only through the death of the old sinful person we were, and the resurrection of a brand new person "created in righteousness and true holiness;" only then, will we be married to Jesus Christ, and bring forth fruit unto God. Our union with, or marriage to Christ means that we receive His "name," or identity which is, among others, the Righteous One. It is our union with Him that makes us righteous and, therefore, capable of bringing forth fruit unto God.

The effects of the believer's death to the law are further explained in verses 5 and 6. Under the law the natural man is found guilty and condemned to death. As stated before by Paul, the law was added to magnify sin, (Romans 5:20), thereby driving us to faith in Christ for salvation (Galatians 3:22,23). Paul refers to this function of the law when he states that under its dominion the sinful "motions" or impulses energized our bodies to "bring forth fruit unto death". This simply means that the bondage of the law actually increases our awareness of sins, *and also, the sins themselves.* In short, the bondage of the law increases our service to sin for "the strength of sin is the law" (1 Corinthians 15:56)

In contrast to the bondage of the law and sin, Paul next describes the effects of our death to the law. Having died with Christ, we died to the bondage of sin and, therefore, to the law which seeks to magnify sin. Where there is no sin, there is no need for law to expose that sin.

Romans 7:4

In the same way, my friends, you have died to the law through the body of Christ, so that you may belong to another, to him who has been raised from the dead in order that we may bear fruit for God." (nrsv)

Dead to the Law

Alpha Series
Who Shall Deliver Me?

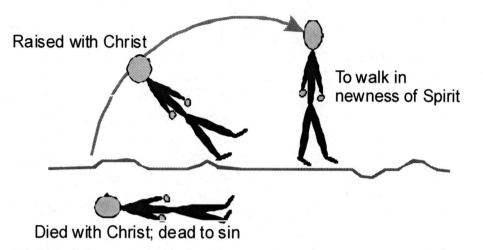

We are dead to both sin and the law, therefore we are now free to serve God "in newness of Spirit, and not in the oldness of the letter". Paul means our death to the law enables us to yield our members as servants of righteousness in the power and leadership of the Holy Spirit. We can now rely fully upon the inward power and motivation of the Holy Spirit instead of looking to an external set of rules and regulations to govern our lives.

The Purpose of the Law

In verses 7-13 Paul reveals the deadly interplay between the law and sin. His main purpose here is to demonstrate the function of the law in exposing sin, and arousing it to such an uncontrollable state that we have no choice, but to turn to Jesus to save us. When the law is applied, sin is not only revealed, but also viewed as being "exceedingly sinful". This simply means that the law brings us to the realization that we are powerless to save ourselves in any sense.

The purpose of the law
To reveal your personal need for a savior

By giving the law God not only intended to protect and preserve His people as a group, but also *to reveal their individual need for a savior*. The function of any law system is always to preserve the integrity of the group. Without law we would soon have no group or society. *That useful purpose for the group, however, is not the same for the individual.* The law was never intended by God to be a means of salvation for the individual, it was a means to protect the group. When we try to use the law to save ourselves we fall into a self-centered trap of manipulation and self-deceit. We will become either proud or despondent. The law can only demand absolute righteousness, and condemn to death those who fail to meet its de-

Dead to the Law

Alpha Series
Who Shall Deliver Me?

mands. It is useful to the individual only in the sense that it points out our helplessness, and need for a savior.

In pointing out our desperate need for a savior, the law does serve an important function in our lives. However, *when we turn to Christ in faith, the purpose of the law is fulfilled,* and we must, then, learn to live our lives by grace through faith in our union with Christ. Once the purpose of the law is served in our lives, it has no more purpose; it has done its job.

In the studies to follow we shall explore the way we may "serve in newness of the Spirit, and not in the oldness of the letter". In order to do so, however, we must first give up our natural tendancies to save ourselves by keeping the law. We must believe that we are as dead to the law as we are to sin.

Romans 7:7-13

The knowledge of sin

⁷ You might think I am saying that sin and the law are the same thing. That is not true. But the law was the only way I could learn what sin meant. I would never have known what it means to want to take something belonging to someone else if the law had not said, 'You must not want to take your neighbor's things.'"
⁸ And sin found a way to use that command and cause me to want all kinds of things I should not want. But without the law, sin has no power."
⁹ I was alive before I knew the law. But when the law's command came to me, then sin began to live,"
¹⁰ and I died. The command was meant to bring life, but for me it brought death."
¹¹ Sin found a way to fool me by using the command to make me die."
¹² So the law is holy, and the command is holy and right and good."
¹³ Does this mean that something that is good brought death to me? No! Sin used something that is good to bring death to me. This happened so that I could see what sin is really like; the command was used to show that sin is very evil. *(ncv)*

Alpha Series
Who Shall Deliver Me?

QUESTIONS

CHAPTER SEVEN: WHO SHALL DELIVER ME?

Lesson One: Dead To The Law

1. What analogy does Paul use in Romans 7:1-4 to illustrate the principle of being dead to the law?

2. What are examples of types of law?

3. What is it about these laws and all laws that we find it necessary live up to all our lives?

4. What is God's solution to the problem of our attachment to the law? (See Romans 6:6-10 and relate your answer to the analogy in question one).

5. What is the purpose of our being freed, through death, to the law?

6. What is the purpose of the law?

7. What is the relationship between law and sin?

Alpha Series
Who Shall Deliver Me?

WHO SHALL DELIVER ME?
CONFLICT WITHOUT CONDEMNATION

Chapter 7 • Lesson 2

A Poor Self-Image

At times all of us suffer from a negative or poor self-image. Due to circumstances or relational problems, we begin to view ourselves as being less secure or significant as a person. Such was the case for the apostle Paul as he wrote Romans 7:14, "For we know that the law is spiritual, but I am carnal, sold under sin." After describing how the righteous demands of the law aroused sin in his life, Paul naturally began to think of himself as "...carnal, sold under sin." In the terms we've been using in this series, *Paul saw himself as being worthless due to the sin exposed in his life by the law.*

In this study we will examine the inward struggle that every Christian, including the apostle Paul, experiences on a daily basis. Although there are seasons when the struggle may seem more or less intense, each of us must contend with this inner turmoil in one way or another. Paul's testimony in the latter verses of Romans 7 reveal the manner in which we should apply the gospel to the conflict within us. He shows us the proper view, and understanding of this conflict.

Mistaken Identity

The source of Paul's negative self image is explained in verse 15 as having to do with his poor performance as a Christian. He says first that he is confused about his own behavior. "For that which I do I allow not" is Paul's way of saying I don't understand myself in terms of my performance. This same personal confusion underlies such common statements as, "I just don't understand why I said that," or "I can't figure out why I acted that way when I really know better". His confusion about his own behavior is the source of his poor self-image because he is naturally believing that his worth as a person is based upon his performance. He further states, "...for what I would, that do I not; but what

> **Improper views**
>
> An *improper* view of the conflict focuses on our performance and not on our identity.
>
> ———————————
>
> An *improper* view of the conflict views our worth as a person to be based upon our performance
>
> ———————————
>
> An *improper* view of the conflict believes we can actually determine our performance
>
> ———————————
>
> An *improper* view of the conflict believes We are dead to God, and alive to

Conflict Without Condemnation

Alpha Series
Who Shall Deliver Me?

Proper view

A proper view of the conflict recognizes the internal desire to do good is from the New Man, motivated by the Spirit and not doing it is the residual effect of the human sin nature left behind after the death of the Old Man

I hate, that do I..." meaning that he has lost control over his own behavior so that he can not make himself behave.

In verse 16 he focuses his attention on his desires, or will, rather than his behavior. It is this subtle shift in his attention that suggests that he is beginning to recall, and apply the gospel he had written down earlier in Romans. *Apparently Paul had lost sight of, and quit relying upon the fact that he was dead to sin, and alive unto God,* (Romans 6:11), while looking at the effect of the law on his life. His statement that he was "carnal, sold under sin", implies that he was thinking of himself as being dead to God, and alive unto sin. But in verse 16 he notes that if he does not really want to do what he is doing, that he is, at least, consenting to the goodness or rightness of the law even though he cannot actually practice it.

All Christians must grasp the realization, it is our true identity that counts in spite of our poor performance.

As Christians, our performance is often very poor and carnal

He is saying that deep down inside he knows what is right, and what he ought to do; and that he, himself, really wants to do what is right according to God's law. *Meager and weak as this may seem to be, it is of utmost importance that we recognize Paul's inward desire to do what is right as the yearning of a new creature to be what God has made him to be.*

In the middle of his struggle to do what is right Paul begins to see that he has a desire to do what's right. It is at this point that he probably recalled the command of Romans 6:11 to count on the fact that he was dead to sin, and alive unto God. His desire to do God's will was evidence that he was still a brand new creature who was dead to sin in spite of his outward behavior. All Christians must grasp the same realization, it is our true identity that counts in spite of our poor performance. We must learn to quit basing our worth on our own ability to behave ourselves, and realize that we are worthy because of who God has made us to be in Christ. In short, we must trust the Word of God more than our own performance for our worth.

We must trust God's word rather than our performance or behavior

Paul's conflict is echoed in the experience of all Christians who are serious about their new life in Christ. When we set out to truly live the supernatural life of Christ, we immediately discover a conflict raging within. We know that we should love others as Christ loves them, (John 13:34,35); pray without ceasing, (1 Thes. 5:17); not be weary in well doing, (Gal. 6:9); think of others more than ourselves, (Phil. 2:2-4); and never worry, (Phil. 4:6). Note, all are New Testament "do's and do not's," and are easily taken legalistically. But, the truth is, in spite of our strongest desire to live this supernatural life, *we*

Alpha Series
Who Shall Deliver Me?

often find that we hate others, go weeks without really praying, grow bone tired of serving, ignore the needs of others because of our own problems, and worry about even the smallest things. When we are really honest with ourselves, we too may recognize that we are yet "carnal, sold under sin," and develop a poor self-image. It is at this point that we lose sight of the gospel of Romans 6, and fail to really count on the fact that we are dead to sin, and alive unto God. Like Paul, then, we too must recognize that the inward desire to do what is right is proof that we are still slaves to righteousness —inwardly at least.

The Distinction in Identity

In verses 17-20 Paul makes an important distinction between his true identity as a believer in Jesus Christ, and the nature of indwelling sin. In the figure below this distinction is illustrated by the difference between the inner and outer triangles within the same circle.

Paul declares that it is not really his true self that behaves inappropriately by violating the law of God. The real Paul is a new creation, (2 Cor. 5:17), created in Christ Jesus unto good works, (Eph. 2:10), and does not commit sin, (1 John 3:9). Therefore, it is not the real Paul that violates God's law, but sin, (the flesh), that yet dwells within his physical body.

The former Paul, as a natural descendant of Adam, was put to death; crucified with Christ. But, the conditioning influences of that Old Man (sin), still remains rooted and imbedded deep within his subconscious mind. It is the sinful thinking (false assumptions), emotions, and habits of the flesh that keep the real Paul from doing what is right.

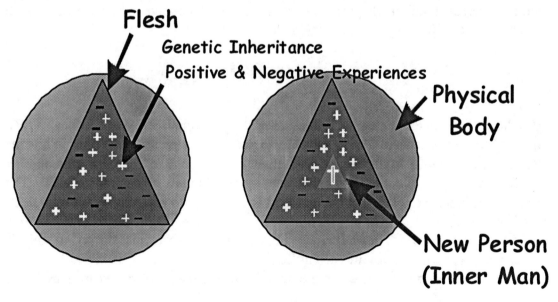

Conflict Without Condemnation

Next, Paul states that he knows there is nothing good in his flesh (the old sin nature). He knows this because even though he wants to do good, he can not make himself do it. The good that he chooses to do he can't do, and the evil he chooses to avoid, he does. Such a contradiction between Paul's will and his behavior is evidence, again, that there is a distinction between his true identity in Christ and the flesh that still surrounds him. This distinction is in keeping with the facts presented in Romans 6:6 and 6:17 concerning our true identity.

It is important to note that the distinction between the new identity and the flesh is not in any sense an excuse for sinning, avoiding the consequences of sin in our lives. We may say with Paul that "it is no more I that do it, but sin that dwelleth in me," but such a statement will not, by itself, eliminate our sin problem, or its consequences in our lives. Making a distinction between our true identity in Christ and our sinful flesh requires a personal faith in the gospel that will give us the courage to be honest about our flesh rather than simply excusing, or trying to cover it.

> **The distinction between who you were and who you are**
>
> **Romans 6:6**
>
> *We know that our old life died with Christ on the cross so that our sinful selves would have no power over us and we would not be slaves to sin.* (ncv)
>
> **Romans 6:17**
>
> *But thanks be to God that you, having once been slaves of sin, have become obedient from the heart to the form of teaching to which you were entrusted,* (nrsv)

The Need For Deliverance

In the closing verses of chapter 7, Paul states the general principle of conflict. Whenever he (the new man in Christ) wants to do good, evil is present with him. While the real Paul "delights in the law of God after the inward man", he also sees another principle in his body (i.e. the flesh), that wars against the law he desires to fulfill. The result of this inner turmoil is that the real Paul is brought into captivity by his own flesh. *Paul's own will power, even as a new creature in Christ, is not sufficient to save him from the habit, and power of sin in his life.* It is impossible for him to "just say no" to sin. He is in essence a prisoner to his own sinful flesh.

Because he recognizes the complete inability of his own will power to obey God's

Alpha Series
Who Shall Deliver Me?

law, Paul cries, "O wretched man that I am! Who shall deliver me from the body of this death?" (verse 24). This question is a key question, one to which each person must come before delivery from the dominion of sin can begin to occur. This question makes it clear that Paul realized his own need for someone *to do for him what he could not do for himself.* He was not saved from the guilt and penalty of sin by his own efforts, and neither will he be saved from the habit and power of sin by his own efforts. So he cries out for a *person* to save him from the habit and power of sin. It is only by the grace of God through the person and work of Jesus Christ that we may be delivered *from the bondage of our own flesh.*

> **The general principle of conflict**
>
> I know what is right, but I do not do it and I cannot stop doing what I know is wrong!

Paul ends the chapter with a summary statement of the conflict within all true believers, "So then with the mind I myself serve the law of God, but with the flesh the law of sin." If we were to stop our study at this point, we might get the idea that such a conflict means our worth as persons is reduced because we have this inner turmoil. The first verse of the next chapter, however, offers great assurance to all who experience a conflict within. The word, "therefore" in this verse connects the inner conflict with a promise that we are under no condemnation by God. This means that the experience of conflict between our new person and the flesh is not a sign that we are worthless, but rather, we are, indeed, *worthy,* and under no condemnation. Rather than being a bad thing to be avoided or covered, our inner struggle should be viewed as *proof positive that we are new creatures in Christ* who are not condemned just because we struggle against the flesh.

> **We must have someone do for us what we cannot do for ourselves**

> **The need for a Savior** — Romans 7:24
>
> O wretched man that I am! Who shall deliver me from the body of this death? (kjv)

In the next chapter we will again focus our attention on how God, through Christ, delivers us from the captivity of our own flesh. But, for now we should realize so long as we yet live in this physical body with the principle of indwelling sin called our flesh, we will have conflict within us. Rather than taking that conflict to mean we are worthy of condemnation, we are to take it as a sure sign that we *are* new creatures in Christ, and under *no* condemnation. We must learn to face our inner conflict without condemning ourselves, and denying the gospel about who we really are in Christ. We must learn to live beyond our experiences and circumstances; to live beyond the physical realm, and to live in the spiritual realm. We must have faith!

Conflict Without Condemnation

Alpha Series
Who Shall Deliver Me?

QUESTIONS

CHAPTER SEVEN: WHO SHALL DELIVER ME?

Lesson Two: Conflict Without Condemnation

1. What is characteristic of an improper view of the conflict?

2. What is a proper view of the conflict?

3. What is the distinction between your true identity as a believer in Jesus Christ and the nature of indwelling sin? (Read Romans 6:6, 6:17, 1 Peter 1:23 and 1 John 3:9).

4. Describe the trouble Paul was going through that climaxes in Romans 7:24. Describe the way in which this applies to you.

SALVATION BY GRACE — Chapter 8
THE FREEDOM OF THE SPIRIT — Lesson 1

What a relief it is to know that we are under no condemnation as Christians; even in the middle of our struggle against our own sinful impulses of the flesh. *If there is any one message that is needed by the church today, it is the good news that Christians are not guilty, and should not fear the wrath and condemnation of God.* In the eighth chapter of Romans, Paul begins to describe what God is doing about our sin problem,

> **Checklist for mental health**
> ➤ **Daily reading of Romans 8**

which produces a poor self-image, and is the foundation for a dysfunctional lifestyle. The statements he makes early in this chapter are so glorious, and yet unbelievable to the natural mind, care must be exercised for maximum benefit. Two functions must be fulfilled: one—***examine each detail***, and two—***allow time for personal application***. An overview of the content of Romans chapter eight is presented in this lesson, *however, the reader is advised to make Roamns chapter 8 daily reading for personal meditation.*

No Condemnation

Based upon our salvation from the penalty of sin, through faith in Christ, Paul confidently says those who are in Christ Jesus are not under condemnation, rather, they are under grace. Remember what was pointed out in our discussions about Romans 6: all believers have been joined to Christ in His death, burial and resurrection so we might "walk in newness of life." Our "Old Man" was crucified with Him so the body of sin, the body of this death, in Romans 7:24, might be destroyed, and that we should no longer serve sin. Although we were once the slaves of sin, by faith in the gospel we are "made free from sin" (Romans 6:18). The person *we used to be* was put to death, destroyed, so the person *we are now* is no longer compelled to serve sin.

Our union with Christ not only crucified, and buried the "Old Man," but also raised up a "New Man." This "New Man" is never under the dominion of sin and law and, therefore, is not under condemnation. The degree of security we experience is directly proportional to the extent we realize, and

> **Free indeed**
>
> *The believer who recognizes his true identity in Christ as the New Man, who still lives in a sin cursed body, realizes he is not under condemnation despite what he sees and may experience in his body of sin. This realization (the truth) sets him free from the captivity and power of sin to be Christ to others, walking in newness of life.*

Freedom of the Spirit

Alpha Series
Salvation By Grace

The principle of sin

Romans 5:12

> *Therefore, just as sin came into the world through one man, and death came through sin, and so death spread to all because all have sinned– (nrsv)*

The effects of the principle of sin: Captivity

Romans 7:23

> *But I see another law working in my body, which makes war against the law that my mind accepts. That other law working in my body is the law of sin, and it makes me its prisoner. (ncv)*

accept in faith this fact concerning our new position "in Christ." Only when we feel secure enough can we honestly confess our present earthly condition in the flesh. That is, we can be real about the indwelling principle of sin (i.e. the flesh) with ourselves, others, and especially God because we *are* absolutely secure, and not concerned about condemnation fearing we must hide from God. Such confession and realness before God brings home to us, personally, the experience and confession of Paul as he made the transition from Romans 7 to Romans 8. Such a transition is necessary to deliver us from the power of sin, and will be ours as we get real with God. Thus, it is the Spirit of life in Christ Jesus that sets us free from all condemnation.

The basis for freedom

Romans 8:3-4

> ³ *The law was without power, because the law was made weak by our sinful selves. But God did what the law could not do. He sent his own Son to earth with the same human life that others use for sin. By sending his Son to be an offering to pay for sin, God used a human life to destroy sin.*
> ⁴ *He did this so that we could be the kind of people the law correctly wants us to be. Now we do not live following our sinful selves, but we live following the Spirit. (ncv)*

Believers are not under condemnation because they are set free from the principle (law) of sin and death by the principle (law) of the Spirit of life in Christ Jesus. The principle of sin and death was described earlier in Romans 5:12 as having entered the world through Adam's sin which brought death upon all the human race. Everyone is born spiritually dead, and captive to sin. It is summarized in Romans 6:23 by the phrase, *"the wages of sin is death"*, and referred to in Romans 7:23 as, "another law in my members", which brings us "into captivity to the law of sin". It is from this "captivity to the law of sin" that the Spirit of life in Christ Jesus sets us free.

Alpha Series
Salvation By Grace

Specifically the law of the "Spirit of life in Christ Jesus" refers to the miraculous working of the Holy Spirit in each believer. It is the Spirit who regenerates us, (John 3:5-8), immerses us into Christ, (1 Cor. 12:13), seals us, (Eph. 1:13,14; 4:30), and indwells us, (John 7:37-39; 14:17; 1 Cor. 6:19). In short, it is the Holy Spirit who communicates the life of Christ to us, thereby setting us free from the principle of sin and death. The basis for our freedom in the Spirit is described in Romans 8:3-4 as purely the gracious work of God.

Negatively, we are set free from the principle of sin and death because of the lack of power of the law, which can only demand, and condemn. The law cannot bring life and freedom.

More importantly however, because the law could never give life in that it was weak through the flesh, *God sent his own son* in the likeness of sinful flesh to condemn sin in the flesh. When Jesus was made sin for us on the cross, (2 Cor. 5:21), he bore the wrath and punishment of God against all sin in the flesh. *Thus, God maintains justice (condemnation for sin), and mercy (forgiving sin) by justifying the sinner because Jesus paid the full price for sin.*

> **The exchange of sin for righteousness**
> 2 Corinthians 5:21
>
> *For our sake he made him to be sin who knew no sin, so that in him we might become the righteousness of God.* (NRSV)

> **Christ fulfilled the righteous demands of the law**
>
> Jesus took the penalty of sin
>
> Jesus lived the perfect righteous life

Positively, we are set free from the law of sin and death because *Christ fulfilled the righteous demands of the law for us.* He did this in two ways. Not only did he suffer, and die in our stead, but he also lived a completely righteous life in obedience to the will of the Father. *When we receive Jesus Christ we receive the full righteousness demanded by the law in every way.* Thus, on the basis of imputed righteousness (something done for us we could not do for ourselves and accepted by faith) we are set free from the power of sin.

The last phrase of Romans 8:4, "who walk not after the flesh, *but after the Spirit*" refers to our supernatural birth and life in the Spirit described earlier as "newness of life" (6:4); "being slaves to righteousness" (6:18); "being married to another" (7:4); and "serving in the newness of the Spirit" (7:6). Our life in the freedom of the Spirit is characterized by a continual reliance upon the power of the indwelling Spirit (not on our ability) to overcome the power of sin in the flesh.

Freedom of the Spirit

Alpha Series
Salvation By Grace

The Mind of the Spirit

In the next few verses, Paul advances the concept of walking in the freedom of the Spirit rather than the bondage of the flesh. It is worth noting that *he does not focus on behavior or feelings* when contrasting life in the Spirit with life in the flesh. Instead, he tells us that those after the flesh *continually* THINK the things of the flesh while those after the Spirit *continually* THINK the things of the Spirit. The clear implication is that the difference between life in the flesh and life in the Spirit is characterized by the thoughts, beliefs and attitudes held by the individual.

"*After the flesh*" refers to the life characterized by the sinful nature and is synonymous with "walking in the flesh". Paul describes this kind of life earlier in Romans (1:18-32; 3:10-18) and elsewhere in the scriptures (Gal. 5:19-21; Eph. 2:1-3; 4:17-19). Here he simply tells us that the underlying *cause for such a dysfunctional lifestyle is the "mind of the flesh," or false thinking.*

"*After the Spirit*" is characterized by the new nature of Christ and is synonymous with "*walking in the Spirit*". This new life has been described by Paul as the righteous life of Christ imputed to all who believe on Him, (Romans 3:21-24; 5:1-11). It stands in total opposition to the flesh and is characterized by the fruit of the Spirit noted in Galatians 5:22,23. *It is based on continually thinking the things in the mind of Christ, (1 Cor. 2:9-14; Phil. 2:5-8).* The result of each kind of thinking is depicted in a dramatic contrast between life and death. The "mind of the flesh" is said to end in death while the "mind of the Spirit" yields life and peace. In this way, Paul contrasts the two in relationship to God. The carnal (natural) "mind of the flesh" has nothing to do with God, His Son, His Word, His people, etc.; *it is focused on self* and leads to dysfunction or death. It is described in verse 7 as being enmity with God and is not only opposed to God, but *incapable* of keeping His law *and compelled not to do so*. The "mind of the Spirit," however, is in complete harmony with God and is *focused on God*. It can know and receive the things of God and leads to life and peace. By this Paul means that the "mind of the Spirit" is in

> **Lifestyle differences**
> The difference between life in the flesh and life in the Spirit is characterized by the thoughts, beliefs and attitudes held by the individual. Each lifestyle is characterized by what one continually THINKS.

> **The contrast between life and death**
>
> **Walking after the flesh:**
> The cause for such a dysfunctional lifestyle is the mind of the flesh or false thinking
> Focus on self
>
> **Walking after the Spirit:**
> The cause of a truly functional lifestyle is the mind of Christ or true thinking
> Focus on God

Alpha Series
Salvation By Grace

Perceptions and attitudes of the mind		
Your perception of:	THE MIND OF THE FLESH	THE MIND OF THE SPIRIT
God is... Self is... Others is... Trials is...	Foolishness Sinful in Adam Competition Condemnation	Wisdom Righteous in Christ Love Chastening
Your attitude about	Your attitude is:	Your attitude about:
God is... Self is... Others is... Trials is...	Rebellion Worthless Manipulation Victim	Submission Worthy Ministry Victory

From glory to glory

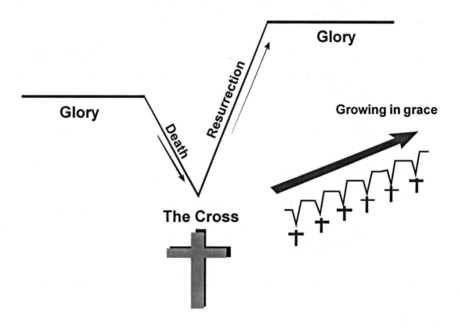

Freedom of the Spirit

complete fellowship with God and shares in all that He is, or has. It is implied that the "mind of the Spirit" fulfills the law of God and pleases Him in contrast to the "mind of the flesh". The table on the previous page illustrates the contrast between the mind of the flesh and the mind of the Spirit.

The Mind of Christ

Of special significance when it comes to the mind of the Spirit is the realization *we have been given the mind of Christ*. As noted earlier, if we are going to live a healthy functional life, we must learn *to base our worth as persons on biblical assumptions of truth*. These are composed of perceptions, thoughts and beliefs that *coincide with the "mind of Christ."* We are assured from the scriptures that we have the mind of Christ (1 Cor. 2:14) and admonished to put it to use (Phil. 2:5). Because our feelings and behavior ultimately originate in our minds, that is in our thoughts, *we must learn to perceive and think like Christ*. Despite what we see as our behavior or performance we must maintain the faith about who God has truly made us to be. We *walk by faith not by sight*. I*n order for our behavior to conform to our true identity, it is essential that the Spirit renew our minds from the inside out.* We are to allow the Spirit to produce in each of us the following characteristics of the mind of Christ:

Philippians 2:5-8

(1) **A TRUE IDENTITY:** Jesus knew who he was, "being in the form of God, thought it not robbery to be equal with God".

(2) **GAVE UP HIS OWN RIGHTS:** Jesus literally emptied himself of all rights to be worshiped as God, "but made himself of no reputation".

(3) **BECAME A SERVANT:** Jesus realized His mission was to minister to others rather than be ministered to, "and took upon him the form of a servant".

(4) **IDENTIFIED WITH SINNERS:** Jesus understood and put himself in the place of those he sought to save, "and was made in the likeness of men".

(5) **HUMBLED HIMSELF:** Jesus thought more of others than he did of himself, "he humbled himself".

Alpha Series
Salvation By Grace

(6) **OBEDIENT UNTO DEATH:** Jesus continually submitted himself to the will of the Father in all he said or did, "became obedient unto death, even the death of the cross".

(7) **EXALTATION BY GOD:** Jesus waited for the Father to exalt Him in due time, "Wherefore God also hath highly exalted Him".

The mind of Christ may be graphically demonstrated to have a positive effect on our personal development and growth by the figure on page 121. Note that the movement from glory to glory always involves the pathway that leads to a time of humiliation and suffering, (the cross). The mind of Christ was willing to go to the cross to complete the Father's plan rather than avoid it for the sake of feeling better. God's uses the same method of maturing us as children... death and resurrection. Death of the old and resurrection of the new over and over again. Repeated cycles of death and resurrection in our lives produces the growth and maturity we need to have the mind of Christ.

Alpha Series
Salvation By Grace

QUESTIONS

CHAPTER EIGHT: SALVATION BY GRACE.

Lesson One: The Freedom of the Spirit

1. After reading Romans 7:23, what can we conclude?

2. Based upon what the believer sees in his life, what should he conclude about his relationship with God?

3. Upon what is the degree of security we experienced based?

4. In being set free from the principle of sin and death, how do we receive the life of Christ?

5. What is the difference between "walking in the Spirit" and "walking in the flesh?"

6. What is "walking in the Spirit" based upon?

7. How do we get the "mind of Christ?"

8. What is meant by progressing from glory to glory?

SALVATION BY GRACE	Chapter 8
THE CALL TO FAITH	Lesson 2

Another Provision: the Power of the Spirit

The apostle Paul directs our attention to the person and work of the Holy Spirit living within each believer by describing the miraculous way that God is delivering His people from the habit and dominion of sin, and all its dysfunction. Having told us that our inner conflict with our flesh is not a sign of condemnation but confirmation of our new identity, he further explains that, "the law of the Spirit of life in Christ Jesus" gives us true freedom and a radically different way of thinking. In Romans 8:9-13, we are given yet another provision of God for our salvation from sin in our every day experience. We are given the resurrection power we need to be delivered from the bondage of our own flesh through the indwelling Spirit of God.

You Are Not Your Flesh But Born of the Spirit

Drawing from all that has been revealed in the previous chapters Paul announces, "But ye are not in the flesh, but in the Spirit..." (verse 9). By this he means that *our identity as persons is no longer to be defined by the historical conditioning of our flesh, but is now determined by the Holy Spirit who lives within each believer.* It was the Spirit who convinced us that we needed a savior,

> **Romans 8:9-13**
>
> 9 But you are not in the flesh; you are in the Spirit, since the Spirit of God dwells in you. Anyone who does not have the Spirit of Christ does not belong to him.
> 10 But if Christ is in you, though the body is dead because of sin, the Spirit is life because of righteousness.
> 11 If the Spirit of him who raised Jesus from the dead dwells in you, he who raised Christ from the dead will give life to your mortal bodies also through his Spirit that dwells in you.
> 12 So then, brothers and sisters, we are debtors, not to the flesh, to live according to the flesh–
> 13 for if you live according to the flesh, you will die; but if by the Spirit you put to death the deeds of the body, you will live. (nrsv)

The Call to Faith

Alpha Series
Salvation By Grace

> **John 3:3**
>
> *Jesus answered him, Very truly, I tell you, no one can see the kingdom of God without being born from above.* (nrsv)

called us to faith in Christ, crucified the "Old Man," and raised up a "New Man," immersed us into Christ, sealed us unto the day of redemption, and lives within us continually. We are no longer identified in the flesh because of this miraculous working of the Holy Spirit, in the new birth. We are brand new persons, "born of the Spirit", with a brand new identity that is radically different from that of the flesh.

> **Identity**
>
> The Christian is re-born; born anew from above; a new creature the New Man

Paul goes on to tell us that all this is either true of us as Christians or we are not Christians at all. Too many people have the idea that they can be a worthless Christian, that they can trust Jesus, but not have this miraculous working of the Holy Spirit in them. Because the crucifixion of the "Old Man" is foreign to our experience (living by sight not by faith), many Christians continue to think of themselves as being the old persons they have been all their lives. They think living the Christian life is like turning over a new leaf. They think they should just try a little harder. They continue to be legalistic, and cling to their own behavior as the means of grace. Although they may have experienced some sort of emotional release when they first trusted Jesus, they soon return to their old ways of thinking, and feeling, and behaving because they have not yet learned about their new identity as the children of God. They do not understand the radical change that has occurred! New Christians have no more understanding of who they really are, than a new born baby has at its birth. It is for this reason that Peter tells us to "desire the sincere milk of the Word (i.e. all that the Father has made us to be in Christ by His Spirit) so we may grow up in Him. Paul now tells us, if you are a Christian, the Spirit of Christ is living in you to give you life and true righteousness.

Resurrection Power

Paul reveals the source of the power we need to overcome the sin nature of the flesh that wars against us (verse 11). He says we are promised that the same Spirit that raised up Christ Jesus from the dead, will continually work in us making our mortal bodies come alive with resurrection power. Our helpless condition, revealed back in Romans 7 as a prisoner to our own flesh is dealt with by the resurrection power of the Holy Spirit now living within the new persons we are. Just as Jesus was raised up from the tomb by the Holy Spirit nearly 2000 years ago, so also that same Spirit is living within us to overcome the death producing power of sin in our flesh. There is no death, dysfunction, or sinful condition that the Holy Spirit cannot overcome by resurrection power.

Paul's conclusion, then, is that we are no longer "debtors to the flesh to live after the flesh." The resurrection power of the Spirit within us is far superior to the power of the flesh. Just as sin and death could not hold Jesus in the tomb when the Spirit raised him from the dead, our sinful nature of the flesh will not be able to withstand the resurrection power of the Holy Spirit working out the life of Christ in us. It is the resurrection power of the indwelling Spirit that renews our minds, comforts us emotionally, and empowers us to walk in newness of life. The same Spirit that raised up Christ is living in us, therefore, we are no longer in bondage to the flesh. We are under no obligation to continue in the dysfunctional life-style that makes us miserable, and irritates others around us. We no longer have to do the things we really don't want to do anymore or not do the things we really want to do. This is how we overcome the flesh: the resurrection power of the Holy Spirit living within the new person God has made us to be.

Living In The Spirit

The resurrection power of the Spirit is the key to experiencing the abundant life Jesus came to give. It was by that same power that He lived and ministered, died on the cross, and rose again from the dead. Likewise, Paul assures us that "...if ye through the Spirit do mortify the deeds of the body, ye shall live", (verse 13). As we trust in, and utilize the power of the Spirit like Jesus did, we too shall be able to overcome the fleshly nature of sin and experience the abundant, eternal life of Christ.

Resurrection power in the Spirit is the key to experiencing the abundant life

The only effective way to control the influence of the flesh upon the body is through the power of the Spirit. The phrase "do mortify the deeds of the body" spells out our responsibility, and needs to be carefully understood. Literally, this phrase means that we are to put to death the practices of the body that are controlled by the flesh. The Greek verb for "mortify" is written in the present tense (implying continual action) and the active voice (meaning action done by us). Thus, it is our responsibility to keep on putting to death the deeds of the body controlled by the flesh, (see also Col. 3:5-9).

Paul does not simply command us to mortify the deeds of the body, and end it there;

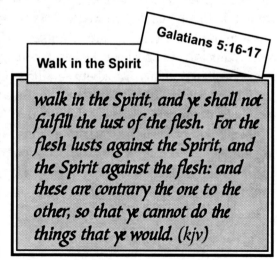

Walk in the Spirit — Galatians 5:16-17

walk in the Spirit, and ye shall not fulfill the lust of the flesh. For the flesh lusts against the Spirit, and the Spirit against the flesh: and these are contrary the one to the other, so that ye cannot do the things that ye would. (kjv)

Alpha Series
Salvation By Grace

that would be like telling us to "just say no to sin!" In so doing, he would again place us under a law system, and our experience would be the same as his in the latter part of Romans 7... "O, wretched man that I am! Who shall deliver me from the body of this death?" Instead, he tells us to mortify the deeds of the body "**by means of the Spirit**". It is only by the personal leadership and supernatural power of the Holy Spirit that we stop doing dysfunctional things. Our responsibility may be summarized in one word —FAITH. We need to trust the personal leadership of the Holy Spirit to both reveal what should be changed in our lives, and to give us the power to change it. The responsibility of the Spirit is to give us the leadership, and power to change.

In Galatians 5, Paul reveals the same basic truth concerning life in the Spirit. After warning us against jumping into some sort of self-improvement plan to make ourselves acceptable to our religious peers, he tells us that we, through the Spirit, are to wait for the hope of righteousness by faith (Gal. 5:5). This means that we are to trust the Spirit to tell us what needs to be changed in us to live out the righteous life of Christ. Rather than submit ourselves to some sort of religious set of rules and regulations, we are to wait on the personal leadership of the Holy Spirit to direct us in what we do or do not do. He explains in the following verse (Gal. 5:6) that what really counts with God is not what we do or do not do (circumcision), but rather our faith which will continually produce in us the divine love we need to relate to others in a healthy way.

One of the biggest problems with Christianity today is so many are engaged in their various self-improvement programs that they cannot think about, or relate to, much less love one another. It is still self-oriented. To live by the Spirit means we stop watching our behavior, constantly wondering what is right and what is wrong or deciding what is right and what is wrong, and start listening to the Holy Spirit for direction.

In Gal. 5:16-17, Paul emphasizes our need for the Spirit with the promise, "walk in the Spirit, and ye shall not fulfill the lust of the flesh. For the flesh lusts against the Spirit, and the Spirit against the flesh:, and these are contrary the one to the other, so that ye cannot do the things that ye would." As we rely in faith on the personal leadership of the Spirit in our daily lives, we are promised that we will not fulfill the lust of the flesh. The reason this is true is because the battle here is not really between us, and our own flesh as it was back in Romans 7, but between the Holy Spirit and our flesh. It is God's battle. The table on the following page shows the difference between fighting the flesh on our own (self-reformation) and trusting the Spirit of God to fight our flesh, (living in the Spirit).

More will be said about what it means to walk in the supernatural power of the Spirit in later lessons. But for now, it is enough to realize that our deliverance from the flesh, and all its dysfunction, is only possible by the grace of God through our faith in the resurrection power of His Spirit.

Alpha Series
Salvation By Grace

Responding to the Pressures of Life by Self Effort verses Spirit Effort

For the following factors we respond one way or another:	SELF EFFORT	SPIRIT EFFORT
	SELF-REFORMATION (Romans 7:15-25)	LIVING IN THE SPIRIT (Galatians 5:16,17)
CONFLICT	Human will vs. Flesh	Holy Spirit vs. Flesh
REALM	Under law	Under grace
FAITH	Rely on will power	Rely on Spirit
RESULTS	Works of flesh	Fruit of Spirit
OUTCOME	Defeat - Bondage	Victory - Liberty

The Call to Faith

Alpha Series
Salvation By Grace

QUESTIONS

CHAPTER EIGHT: SALVATION BY GRACE.

Lesson Two: The Call To Faith

1. In very specific terms how and how not should our identity be determined?

2. When we cling to what we think we should do for God, what term is applied to that thinking and behavior?

3. What is the source of the power we need to overcome the sin nature of the flesh that wars against us? (Romans 8:11). How do we live out the Gospel? How is living as a Christian done?

4. How does Galatians 5:16-17 apply?

THE COMFORT OF THE SPIRIT — Chapter 9
PERSONAL ASSURANCE OF THE SPIRIT — Lesson 1

What made Jesus so healthy and able to function so well in this world? It was the personal assurance and leadership of the Holy Spirit. Beginning with His conception in Mary's womb, and through His resurrection from the tomb, Jesus was empowered by the Spirit of God to say and do all things necessary to fulfill the Father's plan. By His own testimony He did nothing of himself, but rather, led by the Spirit, *He did all, and only* what the Father required. It was the miraculous and supernatural working of the Holy Spirit, in and through Him, that enabled Jesus to complete His ministry in this world.

How does this apply to us? Remember, everything that is true of Jesus is true of you. Look at Paul's experience. After describing His agonizing struggle with indwelling sin in Romans 7, Paul reveals the marvelous way that God provides for our deliverance from the habit and power of sin and dysfunction through the work of the Holy Spirit. We are under no condemnation, free from guilt, free from feeling guilty, free from fear, able to face God with boldness and confidence, and fully equipped. The mind and power of the Holy Spirit that influenced, and led Paul is in each of us as well. This same Spirit that assured and led Jesus and Paul, now lives in all who accept Jesus as their personal savior. It is to the supernatural working of the Holy Spirit that we now turn attention.

> **Identity** — Romans 8:14-17
>
> *14 For all who are led by the Spirit of God are children of God.*
> *15 For you did not receive a spirit of slavery to fall back into fear, but you have received a spirit of adoption. When we cry, "Abba! Father!"*
> *16 it is that very Spirit bearing witness with our spirit that we are children of God,*
> *17 and if children, then heirs, heirs of God and joint heirs with Christ–if, in fact, we suffer with him so that we may also be glorified with him.* (NRSV)

Personal Leadership

In Romans 8:14-17, Paul describes the personal assurance each one of us may receive from the indwelling Spirit of God. He begins by the simple statement that "as many as are led by the Spirit of God, they are the sons of God," (verse 14), meaning the "adult children of God" are the ones led by the Spirit. The use of the Greek term "huios" (sons)

Alpha Series
The Comfort of the Spirit

indicates that believers are not to relate to God as immature and helpless babes, but as full grown adult children and heirs. All who follow the personal leadership of the indwelling Spirit will relate to God as adult children and heirs to the kingdom. They are motivated by an inward love and devotion (grace) rather than an external set of rules and regulations (the law). They are motivated by knowing who they are, where they stand, and the glory they have in Christ. By equating the personal leadership of the Holy Spirit with the adult-child status, Paul implies we live and act like adult children of God because we have been given the Spirit of His Son who leads us to know and accept our status.

> **Galatians 4:6-7**
> **Child and heir**
> 6 *And because you are children, God has sent the Spirit of his Son into our hearts, crying, "Abba! Father!"*
> 7 *So you are no longer a slave but a child, and if a child then also an heir, through God.* (nrsv)

Since our conduct cannot be controlled by the law, (an external set of rules and regulations), we must be governed internally by grace through the personal leadership of the Holy Spirit. This very thing God promises to do for all who receive His son Jesus as their personal savior. But how do we know He is leading us? Can we really trust Him in all areas of our lives? Does He really care about us personally? These and many other questions tend to cause us to doubt the reality of being led by the Spirit, so Paul assures us in these verses that we are, in fact, being led by the Spirit.

> **Personal guidance**
> *We are speaking here of a personal kind of leadership of the Holy Spirit, not some kind of generic or general guidance. We are talking about the Holy Spirit guiding and leading us, you and me, specifically, individually, and constantly in every matter of life.*

Note, we are speaking here of a *personal* kind of leadership of the Holy Spirit, not some kind of generic or general guidance. We are talking about the Holy Spirit guiding and leading us, you and me, specifically, individually, and constantly in every matter of life.

In order to understand how we are led personally by the Spirit, we must also understand how we can hear personally from God. Jesus said, "My sheep hear my voice, and I know them, and they follow me..." (John 10:27). Hearing the voice of Jesus is necessary to follow His leadership. It is for this very reason that He promises that He would not leave us comfortless in this world, but would come to us through His Spirit living within (John 14:16-18).

Three factors need to be considered when trying to understand the way we hear from God. First, we must realize that since God has given us the ability to think, He will naturally speak to us in the privacy of our own hearts or minds. As the prophet Elijah noted, it is not in the loudness of cataclysmic events, but rather the still small voice within

Alpha Series
The Comfort of the Spirit

The key factor that we shall hear God. The voice of God through the indwelling spirit will frequently appear in a spontaneous flow of persistent thoughts in our minds. This does not rule out the possibility of a neon sign in the sky, or a thunderous roar like the ocean, but most likely it will be a persistent thought repeated over and over in our minds.

> **The key factor**
> Hearing God speak to you in a personal way, by name, specifically, and individually, is the key factor in being personally led by the Spirit

Persistent thoughts, however, are not enough to really discern the voice of Jesus. It is quite possible to have persistent thoughts in our minds that are not of God, as in the case of certain obsessions. This underscores the necessity for filtering our thoughts through the written Word of God, the Bible. This miraculous book was inspired and preserved by God so that we might be aware of how he speaks to us, and what he is concerned about in general. The same Spirit who inspired the forty different men to write the various books and letters of the Bible over 1600 years,

> **Hearing God personally**
> 1. He speaks to us in the privacy of our own hearts or minds in our thoughts. He often uses a persistent thought repeated over and over.
> 2. Our thoughts must be filtered through the written Word of God.
> 3. The circumstances of our lives will accommodate His will. He opens doors, and he closes doors.

will also guide each reader into a proper understanding and personal application of the scriptures. Thus, the written Word of God should be used as a safeguard against the thoughts and intents of the heart that are opposed to God, (Hebrews 4:12).

Circumstances also play a role in hearing God's voice, and following the leadership of the Spirit. Whatever God leads us to do, He will arrange the circumstances of our lives to accommodate His will. For the believer, nothing is left to chance, or is simply a coincidence. Although it's much easier to look back on the circumstances of our lives, and see how God has led us

> **The catalyst: Faith**
> To hear God's voice or follow His leadership, we must trust:
> (1) God exists
> (2) God is speaking to us and will lead us.

(hindsight is always 20/20) we may be assured that He is continually "ordering the steps of the righteous." Our own thoughts, and the written Word of God, combined with our circumstances in life constitute the main factors we need to consider in determining God's leadership.

However, these three factors alone cannot truly reveal God's voice, and leadership in

Personal Assurance of the Spirit

Alpha Series
The Comfort of the Spirit

our lives. The bottom line in this issue, as with all others in the Christian life, is FAITH. "But without faith it is impossible to please Him: for he that cometh to God must believe that He is, and that he is a rewarder of them that diligently seek him" (Hebrews 11:6). In hearing God's voice, or following His leadership, we must trust (1) that God exists, and (2) that God is speaking to us, and will lead us. Only when we believe that God is leading us will we be able to follow His leadership.

The Spirit of Adoption

Besides the failure to trust that God really is leading us, another great obstacle stands in our way of hearing His voice, our fear. *Often we are afraid of what God might say to us if He did speak to us personally.* While the "fear of God" is healthy in the sense that we revere Him, and are willing to submit ourselves to Him completely, being "afraid of God" is really an expression of unbelief in God's goodness and infinite love for us. The dictionary lists several meanings to the word "fear." One of those is "To be in awe of." It is this meaning that should be applied. To assure us on this point, Paul reveals that we have not received "the spirit of bondage again to fear, but the Spirit of adoption" (Romans 8:15). The personal leadership of the Holy Spirit in our lives has no potential of "bad" for us. It is not something to dread. Once you understand your legal status before God (your standing as an heir is something He cannot take away, and still be just), there is no reason for fear. The personal leadership of the Holy Spirit is the legal privilege we may enjoy because we are legally adopted into God's family, one with God's only begotten Son, Jesus. Just as the leadership of the Holy Spirit made Jesus healthy and powerful, so we, too, may enjoy the leadership of the Spirit. Far from being something to be feared, such personal leadership of the "Spirit of adoption" is a fantastic opportunity for all who will receive it by faith. To be led and empowered like

> **Fear verses adoption**
>
> We are legally adopted into God's family, one with God's only begotten Son, Jesus. Jesus has no fear, neither should we, we are legal heirs. The full price of adoption (redemption) has been paid. There is absolutely nothing to fear from the personal leadership of the Holy Spirit. The father loves his children and will never allow anything to happen to them that is not good for them.

> **The sound of God's voice: Assurance**
>
> The first and continuous sound of God's voice will be the assurance of who we are in Christ — children of God and co-heirs with Christ to the kingdom. You are my beloved child in whom I am well pleased.

Alpha Series
The Comfort of the Spirit

Jesus is the way we truly experience the benefits of being in God's family.

Finally, Paul tells us that the Holy Spirit's first and greatest job as the Spirit of adoption is to assure us that we are the children of God. Personally, this means that the Holy Spirit is continually leading us to the knowledge of our new life in Christ with all its security and significance. Because we are the children of God, we are "heirs of God" and "joint heirs with Christ." Every day the Holy Spirit will be speaking to us in our minds, through his written Word and in our circumstances to assure us that we are the adopted children of God who can never be disinherited, and will inherit all the blessings of God in Christ. To the extent that we first hear we are worthy heirs of God, we are in a position to receive instruction on what we ought to do, and the power to do it. The Spirit of adoption will always teach us who we are in Christ, assure us in our new relationship to God as heirs, and then show us how to be Christ to others.

The Fullness of the Spirit

The personal leadership of the Holy Spirit may be summarized by the biblical concept known as being filled with the Spirit. In Ephesians 5:18, we are given the command, "and be not drunk with wine, wherein is excess; but be filled with the Spirit." It is written in the present tense so that we understand that being filled with the Spirit is to be a continuous experience as opposed to an occasional or weekly experience of a "religious high." It is also written in the passive voice so that we realize it is not something we may do to ourselves, but rather something that is done to us. Finally, the analogy of being drunk with wine reveals that the filling of the Spirit is a matter of control over our lives. When we choose to believe the Holy Spirit lives within us, and are willing to trust His leadership, we allow ourselves to be controlled, or filled with the Spirit.

> **Ephesians 5:18**
> Do not be drunk with wine, which will ruin you, but {let yourselves} be filled {continuously} with the Spirit. (ncv)

> **Grieving the Spirit** - Ephesians 4:30
> Is following our own plans and ideas rather than listening to and following the Spirit.

Two other scriptures warn us against refusing to allow the Spirit to control us. In Ephesians 4:30, we are told literally to "stop grieving the Spirit", and in 1 Thessalonians 5:19, we are commanded to "stop quenching the Spirit." We grieve the

> **Quenching the Spirit** - 1 Thessalonians 5:19
> Is listening to the advice of others without consulting the Spirit.

Personal Assurance of the Spirit

Alpha Series
The Comfort of the Spirit

Spirit when we follow our own plans and ideas rather than listen to, and follow the Spirit. We quench the Spirit when we listen to the advice of others without consulting the Spirit. Instead of naturally grieving or quenching the Spirit we are admonished to "walk in the Spirit" (Gal. 5:16), by relying upon Him to personally lead us in all that we do or say. This does not mean that we cannot consider our own ideas or thoughts, neither does it mean we cannot hear from others; it simply means that we trust the Spirit to lead us personally, and rely upon His assurance, and comfort every day of our lives.

Alpha Series
The Comfort of the Spirit

QUESTIONS

CHAPTER NINE: THE COMFORT OF THE SPIRIT.

Lesson One: PERSONAL ASSURANCE OF THE SPIRIT

1. What is the substance of Romans 8:14-17?

2. What is the key factor in being personally led by the Spirit?

3. What are the three factors that we should consider when trying to understand the way we hear from God?

4. What must we do to hear God's voice or follow His leadership?

5. How does the Spirit of adoption offset the fears we have in listening to God—i.e. thoughts that make us fear God will have us do something radical that we do not want to?

6. In hearing personally from God what is the first thing you must hear, and hear every day? Without hearing this you cannot hear from God.

7. What is being "filled with the Spirit?" (See Ephesians 5:18).

8. What is "grieving the Spirit?" (See Ephesians 4:30).

9. What is "quenching the Spirit?" (See 1 Thessalonians 5:19).

Alpha Series
The Comfort of the Spirit

THE COMFORT OF THE SPIRIT — Chapter 9
FACING TRIALS IN THE SPIRIT — Lesson 2

The real test of our faith in the gospel of Jesus Christ always involves personal suffering. Nothing causes us to doubt our worth as persons as much as the personal trials we are called upon to endure in this world. This is why Paul closes his "gospel for believers" with a section devoted to suffering and trials.

In the first half of Romans 8, Paul reveals the glorious gospel of God's provisions in the Spirit to set us free from the habit and power of sin. Based upon our union with Christ, we are under no condemnation, and are free from guilt, free from feeling guilty, free from fear, able to face God with boldness and confidence, and fully equipped. We enjoy the blessings of the freedom, mind, power, leadership and assurance of the Holy Spirit. Since we are the adopted children of God, we are joint heirs with Christ. What a glorious privilege to be one with Jesus!

> **Romans 8:17**
> *And if children, then heirs, heirs of God and joint heirs with Christ–if, in fact, we suffer with him so that we may also be glorified with him. (nrsv)*

In the middle of verse 17, however, Paul introduces the fact that we are joint heirs with Christ "if so be that we suffer with him, that we may be also glorified together." He connects our glory and rejoicing in Christ with our suffering with Him. Our wonderful union with Christ involves His sufferings as well as His blessings. In making this connection, Paul raises the one issue that causes us to doubt the gospel we have been studying —personal suffering; and then proceeds to give us some very practical assurance.

Why Me, Lord?

In verses 18-23 of Romans 8, Paul addresses the age old question concerning the reason for our suffering. He introduces this second statement of hope that is based upon all that he has said concerning our union with Christ. Before attempting to understand why we must suffer, it is imperative that we recognize the truth that "...the sufferings of this present time are not worthy to be compared with the glory which shall be revealed in us." This demands an eternal view of our suffering that can only be gained from God's perspective; that is, we must learn to see, by faith, the end result of our suffering at the beginning of it.

In Romans 5:1-5, Paul outlined the benefits of being justified by faith in Jesus. In addition to peace with God, access into His grace, and rejoicing in the hope of our final destiny in glory; he goes on to outline the unique way we may view trials. Instead of

Alpha Series
The Comfort of the Spirit

dreading them, we can glory or rejoice in them knowing that tribulation produces patience, patience produces experience, experience produces hope, and hope never lets us down because God loves us as His own.

When we see our sufferings from the eternal viewpoint of

> **Romans 8:18-23**
>
> *18 The sufferings we have now are nothing compared to the great glory that will be shown to us.*
> *19 Everything God made is waiting with excitement for God to show his children's glory completely.*
> *20 Everything God made was changed to become useless, not by its own wish but because God wanted it and because all along there was this hope:*
> *21 that everything God made would be set free from ruin to have the freedom and glory that belong to God's children.*
> *22 We know that everything God made has been waiting until now in pain, like a woman ready to give birth.*
> *23 Not only the world, but we also have been waiting with pain inside us. We have the Spirit as the first part of God's promise. So we are waiting for God to finish making us his own children, which means our bodies will be made free. (ncv)*

our union with Christ, we can see the end from the beginning, and know that "...the sufferings of this present time are not worthy to be compared with the glory which shall be revealed in us." Whatever we must suffer in this life cannot even be compared to the glory and rejoicing we shall experience throughout all eternity (see 2 Cor. 4:17-18). The very first thing we must realize is, regardless of what the suffering is, and regardless of why we must suffer, *we cannot possibly lose*.

The eternal view
See the end of suffering at the beginning

The very first thing we must realize is this: regardless of what the suffering is, and regardless of why we must suffer, we cannot possibly lose.

Having called us to consider and trust the eternal view of our suffering, Paul goes on to tell us why we must suffer. Essentially he states that we must suffer because we live in a sin-cursed world that is falling apart, and we live in sin-cursed bodies that are falling apart. Living in such conditions guarantees we, like the creation itself, "groan within ourselves" in suffering and pain. While it is true that God could simply take us out of this world, *he has chosen to leave us in these sin-cursed bodies, in a sin-cursed world, as ambassadors for Christ.* We should not be at all surprised, then, when we suffer in this present time.

This chart summarizes the eternal view of suffering revealed in the scriptures.

DO NOT BE SURPRISED (1 Peter 4:12-14)
- Because of union with Christ (John 15:18)
- For the sake of Christ (Phil. 1:27)
- As a testimony to others (1 Peter 3:13)

SEE THE END AT THE BEGINNING (2 Cor. 4:17-18)
- God's love (Romans 5:3-5)
- Joy unspeakable (1 Peter 1:3-9)
- Peaceable fruit of righteousness (Hebrews 12:1-11)
- Spiritual maturity (James 1:2-4)

KNOW YOU CANNOT LOSE (1 John 5:4)
- With trial comes grace (2 Cor. 10:13)
- God is in absolute control (1 Cor. 10:13)
- All things work for good (Romans 8:28)
- More than conquerors (Romans 8:37)

The Deliverance in Hope

Our suffering, our "groaning within ourselves", is tied directly to the concept of the hope of delivery, the "waiting with excitement" that is occurring. Paul assures us in spite of the suffering, which is natural with a broken body and broken creation, we were saved or delivered-in-hope, that is, in the realm of hope. Our salvation (the new life we have, the "New Man," the spiritual seed of Christ) is based upon our faith in Jesus Christ. This faith, in turn, produces a hope in us concerning the future salvation of our bodies and the entire creation. This hope is a joyful, confident expectation of the

Alpha Series
The Comfort of the Spirit

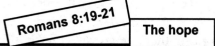

The hope

> ¹⁹ *Everything God made is waiting with excitement for God to show his children's glory completely.*
> ²⁰ *Everything God made was changed to become useless, not by its own wish but because God wanted it and because all along there was this hope:*
> ²¹ *that everything God made would be set free from ruin to have the freedom and glory that belong to God's children. (ncv)*

future.

Obviously, we cannot hope for something we fully perceive now, "for hope that is seen is not hope," (verse 24). By this he warns us against the *false idea* that our salvation guarantees we will not have to suffer. The recent "prosperity gospel," which says if we simply have enough faith we can avoid all suffering, and the reverse—suffering itself is evidence we do not have enough faith, is totally foreign to the scriptures. Instead, our deliverance-in-hope means even though we *must* suffer in this world, we are able to rejoice in hope through the sufferings.

Hope
A joyful, confident expectation of the future

When we are in the midst of sufferings we can joyfully look forward to the coming glorification in faith, and we are able to wait with endurance. The sufferings we endure actually become a source of strength as the Holy Spirit supernaturally produces hope, (a joyful expectation about our future), in our hearts. The ability to patiently endure our sufferings has always been a great testimony to the world about us. Our lives in this world will magnify the character of Christ to the degree we are able to view our sufferings from an eternal point of view. This can only be done because of our union with Christ.

In spite of the suffering which stems from the curse upon the world, we ourselves are saved "by hope". The faith which saved us from the guilt and penalty of sin also places us into the realm-of-hope. The realm-of-hope exists because of the faith in our salvation from the power and presence of sin. This hope enables us to endure the trials of this present world in a more effective manner than those who have no hope. We do not have to waste time and energy trying to avoid trials or complaining and whining about them, hope enables us to face them head on. In the midst of our trials, we can concern ourselves with the welfare of others knowing that, ultimately, we will be delivered.

In the remaining verses of Romans 8, Paul reveals some specific facts concerning the realm-of-hope in which we were saved. The subject of Christian suffering is still addressed, but now from a positive point of view stressing God's provisions for His suffering children. The first, and perhaps greatest provision, is the intercession of the Holy Spirit in time of suffering. Recognizing our natural inability to know fully what we should

Alpha Series
The Comfort of the Spirit

pray for concerning our own or another's suffering, the Spirit continually makes intercession for us. Because we often get our wants and our needs confused, and have only a limited view of our trials, we find it difficult, if not impossible, to express our true desires and feelings. To compensate for our weakness in this area the Holy Spirit continually makes intercession for us with "groanings which cannot be uttered." In other words, the Holy Spirit cries out to the Father on our behalf with words we cannot express.

> **The Realm-of-hope**
>
> Exists because of faith
> Provides joy and peace in the midst of trails
> Enables us to avoid whining and complaining
> Is produced supernaturally by the Holy Spirit
> The Holy Spirit continually intercedes for us in prayer
> Enables us to endure the trials of this present world
> The will of God is accomplished in us despite our suffering
> Involves an eternal point of view

The intercession of the Spirit within us is said to be inexpressible, however, this is from a human view point. God, who searches all hearts, knows the mind of the Spirit; God fully understands the thoughts and feelings expressed by the Spirit, because the Spirit is cooperating with the Father in His intercessory work. This assures us the prayers uttered by the Holy Spirit on our behalf are not only heard, but fully answered so the perfect will of God is accomplished in us in-spite of our suffering.

> **Romans 8:28-29**
>
> 28 *We know that all things work together for good for those who love God, who are called according to his purpose.*
> 29 *For those whom he foreknew he also predestined to be conformed to the image of his Son, in order that he might be the firstborn within a large family.* (nrsv)

In contrast to our inability to know what to pray for, Paul tells us we do know all things work together for our good. No matter what our earthly condition or circumstances, the ultimate purpose of God for each believer is to be conformed to the image of Christ. Regardless of the nature or extent of the suffering involved, it will be worked out for the ultimate good of all who love God, and are "called according to His purpose." It is the plan of God to make each believer like Jesus so that Jesus may receive the glory of being the "first-born among many brethren."

In verse 30 we are given a list of four specific actions of God which describe His overall plan to work all things to our good. He says that we have been predestined, called, justified, and glorified. The use of the aorist tense in each of the Greek verbs tells us these actions occurred once, and for all, at one point in time past. *From the eternal view of God, we were predestined, called, justified, and glorified before the world was created.* We are given this information for personal assurance that all things are working together for our good.

More than Conquerors

In verses 31-39, we reach a glorious climax that gives us a new perspective on suffering. By a series of rhetorical questions, Paul summarizes, proving that we are eternally secure in Christ in spite of our present circumstances. These verses serve to comfort and encourage all who, because of trials, may seriously question God's power, justice, provisions, or love. Paul simply asks what is our response to trials in light of the eternal purpose of God for each believer? Since all things are working to our eternal good according to God's sovereign plan for us, can we say, in any sense, we are going to lose in the face of various trials?

The first of four questions is simply who or what can be against us if God is for us? Since the Creator and God of the universe has already determined to work all things to our good, can anyone or anything possibly be successful against us? The answer is put in the strongest terms possible. Especially when we consider God did not withhold His Son but delivered Him up for us all. Since God gave us the most precious gift of His Son, it is only logical to assume that He will also graciously give us all the things that belong to Him as well.

> **Four acts for our good** — **Romans 8:30**
>
> *And those whom he predestined he also called; and those whom he called he also justified; and those whom he justified he also glorified.* (nrsv)

The next question asks who can accuse us before God? This question frequently plagues the believer when he slips back into thinking of himself as being guilty "in Adam" and, therefore, deserving of punishment. *The only one who has the right to accuse us of anything is the One who has already declared us righteous.*

The next question is

> Who or what can be against us if God is for us?
>
> Who can accuse us before God?
>
> Who can condemn us? (Shall Christ condemn us?)
>
> Who or what can separate us from God's love?

closely related to the last one in that Paul asks who can condemn us? The answer is again in the form of another question that shows how absurd the first one was. Shall Christ condemn us? The One who paid for our sins by his death, and rose again for our justification, and now continually makes intercession for us? The obvious answer is that no one is able to accuse or condemn us.

The last question asks who or what can separate us from God's love? This is especially relevant to all who naturally question God's love in the midst of trials. Paul lists seven types of trials that may be thought to evidence a separation from God's love, and immediately adds a quote from Psalm 44 to emphasize the reality of the suffering of God's children in this world. *The answer is simply that in all these trials we are now and forever "more than conquerors" through God's eternal love.* Regardless of what we must suffer for Christ's sake to bring a lost and dysfunctional world to the gospel, we shall never be separated from the love of God in Christ Jesus our Lord!

Alpha Series
The Comfort of the Spirit

QUESTIONS

CHAPTER NINE: THE COMFORT OF THE SPIRIT.

Lesson Two: Facing Trials In The Spirit

1. What is the significance of Romans 8:18-23 in regard to suffering?

2. In regard to suffering, what is the very first thing we need to realize?

3. What three concepts epitomize the eternal view of suffering?

4. What is the definition of the <u>biblical</u> idea of hope?

5. What is the biblical hope for every Christian?

6. In Romans 8:30, what are the four ideas given which generate hope that all things will work out for good for those who love Christ?

7. In Romans 8:31-39 what are the four rhetorical questions that Paul asks to emphasize our security in Christ? What is the implication?

ANOTHER COMFORTER
RELATIONAL MINISTRY

Chapter 10, Lesson 1

Christianity is not a religion; it is a relationship. A relationship between God and an individual; and a relationship between an individual and others. Conversely, religion is the humanistic attempt of man to somehow manipulate whatever he conceives as deity to bless him, or at least, not curse him. Through legalistic observances of rituals and ceremonies it is hoped that the gods will somehow be appeased and the quality of the individual's life will improve one way or another.

> **The aspects of relational Christianity**
> 1. Vertical: Man and God
> 2. Horizontal: Man and man.

Christianity, on the other hand, is not based upon *personal performance*. Instead, it involves a *personal relationship* between man and God based upon having already received God's blessing by grace through faith alone apart from any human effort.

The expression of such a relationship with God determines the quality of our own personal lives, as well as the quality of our relationships with others. This kind of relationship with God is simply achieved by believing and trusting what God says is true. You have this relationship when you trust in the grace of God, which is expressed in Christ, instead of your ability to appease or please God.

> *Our relationship with God is based upon grace through faith apart from any effort or work by us.*

Up to this point in our series our main concern has been our relationship to God. We have studied the gospel as it applies to our personal needs, and the faith we must exercise in receiving the blessings of God found in His matchless grace. Now, we will examine how this gospel of grace actually impacts our relationships. As we begin to enjoy *personal* health (as expressed in the needs hierarchy explained in chapter two, lesson two "Jesus Meets Our Personal Needs") we can go on to experience relational health as well. We can begin to see our spiritual needs satisfied as we start to express true love for others. The love we receive from our vertical relationship with God may be freely shared in our horizontal relationships with others. Since we have received the love of God by faith in the gospel of Jesus Christ, our own personal needs for worth are fully met. Only then can we realize our full potential to love others as Jesus loves us. In so doing, we are not only addressing our deepest spiritual needs to express divine love, we are actually engaged in the relational ministry revealed by all the "one another" passages in the scriptures.

> *Our relationship with other men is based upon our relationship to God*

Alpha Series
Another Comforter

The Call To Divine Love

In 1 John 4:7-11 we are instructed to engage in the relational ministry of loving others as God loves us. In order to do this, to address our spiritual need to love others like Christ, we must first know that our physical and personal needs are met. All we have studied since chapter two was meant to assure us we *can* trust God to supply *all* of our needs for personal worth as well as physical health. It is now time to apply the gospel, that God has met all of our needs, to our relational ministry with others by beginning to love others like Christ. If we truly believe God has made us worthy because of our union with Christ, then faith will work itself out in an expression of divine love in our relationships.

In commanding we who are "beloved" to love one another, John reveals that the source of love is God who is the very essence of love. The significance of the command "to love one another" being connected to the statement that God is love, is simply meant to illustrate the kind and quality of the love to which John is calling us. It is divine rather than human in its origin and nature. The kind of love that we are to receive from God, and give to others is radically different from what we commonly think of as love in the natural sense.

About relational ministry:
- Opportunities will usually come when we are suffering
- We must know we are secure and significant
- We must love and accept others despite their situation
- It is a call to love, accept, forgive, and restore others

Divine love is unconditional in that it is not given on the basis of merit, but simply because God is love. **God is love** is a very significant point. It is the essence of God's being, and the basis for all we believe. God is love. He cannot change his nature, and he cannot stop loving. God will always be love, and will always love us unconditionally. When he tells us he loves us it is an expression of his very nature, his being. Thus, God's *unconditional* love is as dependable as is the very existence of God. God exists, and so does his unconditional love for us.

The basis for natural, human "love" is the lack of personal worth and the desire to have that security and significance. Conversely, the basis for divine love is absolute personal worth (security and significance) and the knowledge one has it. Since God is absolutely secure and significant **God is love**.

In contrast human love is conditioned upon the response of those it is directed toward. It has, at its core, the need for security and significance. A human being can cease to love, and still be a human. Human love is dependent on having it's need for security and significance met. Looking for security and sig-

> God's unconditional love for us is as dependable as the very existence of God.

nificance, human love says, "I'll love you if you will love me in return." Divine love, with ultimate and absolute security and significance, simply says, "I'll love you." Without absolute security and significance it is impossible to love unconditionally. In Romans 5:8 we are told that God proved His love toward us in that while we were yet sinners (not loving in return) Jesus died for us.

Divine love is *sacrificial* in that its expression involves a cost. It is not cheap, convenient, or stingy, and self-serving as is the humanistic love that says, "I love you," but really means, "I love to be loved by you." In John 3:16 we read, "For God so loved the world that He gave...". Divine love is expressed sacrificially by giving up the most precious thing for the welfare of others. .

Divine love is also *eternal* in nature, meaning that it remains constant, and is consistently expressed. God does not love us more now than He did before, and neither will he love us less in the future. His love is eternal in nature because He, Himself, is unchangeable, and remains the same (James 1:17; Hebrews 13:8).

> 1 John 4:16
> **God is Love**
> And so we know the love that God has for us, and we trust that love. *God is love.* Those who live in love live in God, and God lives in them. (ncv)

Divine love also takes the first step in reaching out to others, and is, therefore, *initiating*. From the sin of Adam in the garden to this present hour God has taken the initiative "to seek, and to save that which was lost." At best, human love, being passive in nature tends to adopt a "wait, and see" attitude, and at worst a "prove it to me" attitude before it responds.

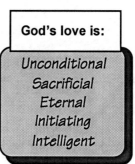

God's love is:
Unconditional
Sacrificial
Eternal
Initiating
Intelligent

Finally, divine love is *intelligent* in that it always does what is best for the one it loves. Rather than do whatever the loved one demands or pleads for, divine love does what is best to ensure their ultimate wellbeing. It is not a syrupy sweet emotion that seeks to win approval from the one loved, but can appear tough and somewhat harsh as it firmly insists on the ultimate best rather than immediate relief. It was divine love that allowed Jesus to suffer the crucifixion so that He might be exalted in surpassing glory later. It is this unconditional, sacrificial, eternal, initiating, and intelligent love of God that we are called to express in our relationships with others.

The Source of Love

After telling us to love others, John immediately points out this love is of God. The kind of love we are called upon to share originates with, and belongs to God. It cannot be received naturally, or expressed by man apart from God. It is the kind of love that is consistent only with God. John goes on to tell us about two prerequisites for being able to love like God.

First, he says we must be born of God. In order to share the love of God we must first share in His nature of love. It is impossible for us to give what we do not have. Without the regenerating work of the Spirit of God in our lives (being "born again"), we cannot truly love others as God does because we have not received that love ourselves. But, when we are "born of God" and *receive His nature of love,* we now have the potential to love others as He does, for we are now "partakers of the divine nature".

Second, it is possible to be born of God (i.e. a Christian) and still not love others like God because we do not know God. By this John means that immature Christians who do not know by personal experience what God has done for them in His great love will not be able to love others like God. Only when we are (1) born of God, and (2) know Him by personal experience as our loving Heavenly Father will we be able to truly love others as He does. As we come to believe in His love meeting our own needs, we are set free to concern ourselves about the welfare of others.

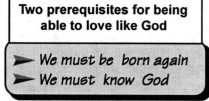

Our Supreme Example

No doubt the greatest display of divine love is found in the relational ministry of Jesus with His disciples in the upper room on the night before He was crucified. In John 13:1-17 we find a marvelous story of Jesus loving His disciples with a divine love to the very end. This example gives us insight into just what it means for us to love one another with the love of God.

Jesus had much to teach His squabbling disciples, and very little time to teach them. So after observing the Passover meal that evening, he gave them an object lesson in relational ministry. He laid aside His outer garments, wrapped a towel around himself like a common house slave, and began to wash their feet. When he had finished washing their feet He asked them if they understood the meaning of this lesson. Understanding this lesson was the key to their happiness in life. By following His example in washing one another's feet rather than fighting with each other, they could experience the comfort and joy of the Spirit that comes only to those who enter into relational ministry.

The same applies to us. Understanding this lesson is the key to our happiness in life. From the example of Jesus' servanthood-ministry, we too may learn several important things concerning our own relational ministries to others. **First**, the greatest opportunity to love others like Jesus will usually come when we are suffering. In the Garden Jesus was able to minister to his disciples despite his own suffering. **Second**, Jesus knew He was secure and significant. Believing the gospel for Himself, Jesus knew "that the Father had given all things into His hands," (significance), and "that He was come from God, and went to God," (security). Trusting that His own needs were met in spite of the dark circumstances about Him, Jesus was free to concern Himself with others. **Third**, Jesus was willing to serve others in humility rather than demand that they serve Him. Jesus showed His disciples divine love in action by washing their feet. In His own divine love he was willing to love and accept them personally, in spite of the defilement of their proud and hateful flesh. His explanation of His actions to Peter meant divine love is always ready to cleanse us from the defilement of our own fleshly nature of sin in this world.

> **Relational ministry**
> - Relational ministry is washing each others feet
> - Relational ministry is loving, accepting, forgiving, and restoring others

> **Divine love**
> - Divine love is washing each other's feet
> - Divine love is loving, accepting, forgiving, and restoring others

Finally, the statement that He has given us an example to follow in washing each other's dirty feet is really a call to the relational ministry of loving, accepting, forgiving, and restoring those who are likewise struggling with the habit and power of sin in their lives. They do not need a judge, they need a savior like Jesus. It is our privilege to represent Christ to others in this world as we engage in the relational ministry referred to here as "ye also ought to wash one another's feet."

Alpha Series
Another Comforter

QUESTIONS

CHAPTER TEN: ANOTHER COMFORTER

Lesson One: Relational Ministry

1. What are the two aspects of relational ministry? Upon what is each based?

2. List some things about relational ministry that we should remember.

3. In 1 John 4:7-11, what is the key concept that triggers and enables relational ministry?

4. What is pivotal in the concept that God is love as expressed in 1 John 4:16?

5. What are five characteristics of God's love?

6. What are the two prerequisites given in order to be able to love like God?

7. What supreme example did Jesus give about relational ministry and what does this illustrate?

ANOTHER COMFORTER — Chapter 10
COMFORT IN RELATIONAL MINISTRY — Lesson 2

Christian Maturity

On the night before Jesus was crucified, He gave His disciples a spiritual heart attack by telling them that He was leaving them. They had been following Him for nearly three years with great personal expectations, and the idea that He would leave them alone in this world was more than they could handle. What would they do now? Where would they go? How would they support and protect themselves? They were all hoping that Jesus would set up an earthly kingdom in which they would be rich and famous. Now their hopes were shattered and they were terrified.

> **John 13:34,35** — The central command for relational ministry
>
> *A new commandment I give unto you, that ye love one another; as I have loved you, that ye also love one another... (kjv)*

Immediately following the startling announcement of His departure, Jesus gave the central command for all relational ministry. "A new commandment I give unto you, that ye love one another; as I have loved you, that ye also love one another," (John 13:34-35). Not only was Jesus leaving them, but, in addition, He expected them to love each other in His absence. Note also *they were to love each other in the same manner that He loved them*, i.e. with a supernatural divine love. This is what made this command to love a "new" commandment. This was brand new —love each other with supernatural love. They were not just to love each other with the humanistic, conditional love they naturally had for themselves, but with His own divine love.

There is no doubt that the disciples were overwhelmed at this time. In fact, it's doubtful any of them even heard the command for relational ministry. Peter's response, "Lord, whither goest thou?" betrays the anxiety in His own mind and heart. His rash promise to lay down his life for Jesus was prompted more out of fear, guilt and pride than love for Jesus. Thus, Jesus predicted Peter would deny Him three times before the night was over. It would be hard to imagine anyone more troubled, depressed, shocked, or grieved than those worried disciples that night. The comfort that Jesus shared with these men is recorded in the fourteenth chapter of John, and is centered around the call to relational ministry issued to all believers. Although much of our study has been devoted to learning what God has done for us in Christ, it is now time to learn what God will do *through us* to love others like Christ. The words of comfort Jesus gave His disciples in the upper room teach us real and lasting comfort comes from the fulfillment of our purpose in learning to love others as He did.

Alpha Series
Another Comforter

The Call To Faith

Jesus began consoling His disciples by calling them to stop focusing on their fears and trust what He was doing for them. He told them His Father's house was big enough for all of them to live together with Him, and He was going away for the express purpose of preparing a place for them to live. Finally, He assured them—if He went away to prepare a place for them, He would certainly return to receive them again. The comfort coming from these words is twofold. First, our separation is only temporary; and second, we will be together with Jesus again. Jesus assures us we will be comforted in the future by living with Him in the Father's house.

His disciples, however, were not so concerned about the distant future as they were the present. Thomas complained he did not know, (by personal experience), where Jesus was going, so how could he possibly know the way there. Like most of us, no doubt, he was assuming responsibility in his own mind for finding the Father's house, and getting back together with Jesus again. Jesus comforted him with a statement that would remind Thomas to trust Him. "I am the way, the truth, and the life: no man cometh unto the Father, but by me," (John 14:6). It is through a personal relationship with Jesus that we may experience the comfort of the Father's house.

> **John 14:6 — The way home**
> *I am the way, the truth, and the life: no man cometh unto the Father, but by me (kjv)*

> *Our relationship with Jesus will meet all our needs*

> *Our relationship with Jesus will empower us to relate to others in ministry*

While catching a glimpse, at least, of what Jesus was saying, Philip said, "Show us the Father, and it is enough for us." Philip meant Jesus should show us something more than just our relationship with him to satisfy our worried hearts. But Jesus mildly rebuked Philip as He reminded him again that if you have seen Jesus, you have seen all the Father has, and is. *What was missing in their experience was not some deeper revelation of God, but simply the faith that their relationship with Jesus was all that they needed to sustain them.* Thus, Jesus called them once again to believe that He and the Father were one. He called them to exercise faith; to believe their relationship with Him was all they needed to meet all their needs.

Alpha Series
Another Comforter

The Promise of Ministry

In verse 12, Jesus makes a shift in thought from the comfort that comes from trusting Jesus to completely satisfy our own needs, to the comfort we receive in actually doing the works of Jesus. Whoever believes in Jesus will not only enjoy the personal security of His love, but will also experience true significance in his ministry. This is what Jesus meant when He promised, "...the works that I do shall he do also; and greater works than these shall he do...," (verse 12). Because of who God has made us to be in Christ, (i.e. slaves of righteousness, able ministers of the new covenant, etc.), we can never be truly satisfied until we are fully engaged in realizing our potential to love others like Christ. This is the highest level of the needs hierarchy (the spiritual need to love) discussed in chapter two. Jesus sought to raise his disciples to this highest level of needs *by directing their attention away from what they might receive toward what they could give.*

The receiving of comfort
- Received by trusting Jesus to meet all our needs (security) - (personal need satisfaction)
- Received when we do the works of Jesus and minister to others (significance) - (spiritual need satisfaction)

The "works of Jesus" encompass all the various ways we may be used by God to minister the gospel to others in our everyday relationships. Although there may be times God would literally cleanse the leper, feed a multitude, give sight to the blind, heal the sick, or raise the dead; it is more likely He will use us to share the gospel with others in our every day lives. As we believe the gospel for ourselves and others in our homes, in school, on the job, or in the community about us, we fulfill the new command to love one another as Jesus loved us. In that process we will see the personal and spiritual impact of "raising the dead"—an impact that is every bit as miraculous as the physical signs and wonders Jesus performed.

The works of Jesus are done in faith

The promise that the believer in Jesus will do "greater works" should be understood in terms of duration of ministry rather than quality. Great as His own earthly ministry was, Jesus only ministered on this earth for about three years. The promise He gives us here is that believers shall surpass that three years by decades. What Jesus began during His ministry the disciples and all who believed the gospel would continue to do for centuries. In other words, we have the unique privilege of not only doing the work of Jesus, but also doing it longer.

In connection with this promise of doing his works, Jesus goes on to assure us that

Alpha Series
Another Comforter

whatever we ask in His name He will do it to glorify the Father (verse 13,14). Jesus does not mean that we may treat Him like some sort of a fairy godmother who grants us wishes. We must understand this promise in the proper context of ministry. It means whatever we ask in identity with Jesus (in union with him, immersed in him, he leading us) for the sake of doing His works, He will do it. In essence this is a guaranteed prayer request for being used by God to effectively minister to others.

It was at this point in His discourse that Jesus first promised the comfort of the Holy Spirit whom He referred to as the Spirit of Truth, and, literally, "another of the same kind of Comforter." In connection with our faith in Christ working itself out in the ministry of loving others, Jesus promises to do all we ask.

He also promised to send us the same kind of comforter He was to His disciples. He knows all about our human frailties and promises to continue to care for us through the presence and indwelling of the Holy Spirit. ***It is by means of His Spirit that Jesus comes to us personally to comfort us as we seek to do His works.*** Nothing in this world can possibly match the comfort that Jesus promises to those who are willing to commit themselves in faith to being Christ to others around them. Truly, He has not left us comfortless, (like orphans), but has come to us through another Comforter, the Holy Spirit.

> **John 14:13**
> *And if you ask for anything in my name, I will do it for you so that the Father's glory will be shown through the Son.* (ncv)

Alpha Series
Another Comforter

QUESTIONS

CHAPTER TEN: ANOTHER COMFORTER

Lesson Two: Comfort In Relational Ministry

1. What is Jesus' central command for all relational ministry? What is so unique and incredible about this command?

2. Jesus told his disciples he was going away and would prepare a place for them in his Father's house. How can we now (before death) experience the comfort of the Father's house? What responsibility do we, as Christians, have for finding the Father's house?

3. Sometimes we do not experience the comfort of the Father. Why not?

4. There is a comfort, called security, that comes from trusting Jesus to satisfy all our needs. What related means is available for receiving this comfort of the Father? In what form is this comfort experienced?

5. How do we "live out the Gospel" in our daily lives?

6. What does Jesus mean in John 14:13 when he says he will give us anything we ask?

Alpha Series
Another Comforter

ABIDING IN CHRIST
THE VINE AND THE BRANCHES

Chapter 11, Lesson 1

The Key to Living As Christ

According to Jesus' own testimony, the key to His miraculous life and ministry as the Son of Man was His union with the Father. On several occasions, Jesus said the words He spoke, and the works He did were due to His being one with the Father, (John 5:19; 8:28; 10:30,38; 14:9-11; 17:21,22). Jesus was given the personal security and significance required to fulfill His ministry and lay down His life for the sake of others, *because He and the Father were inseparably joined by the Holy Spirit.*

Our main purpose in this study has been to discover the gospel—*just as Jesus was one with the Father, we too are one with Him.* As we have

Union with the Father — John

> **5:19** the Son can do nothing alone. The Son does only what he sees the Father doing, because the Son does whatever the Father does.
>
> **8:28-29** You will know that these things I do are not by my own authority but that I say only what the Father has taught me. The One who sent me is with me. I always do what is pleasing to him, so he has not left me alone."
>
> **10:30-38** The Father and I are one."
> I have done many good works from the Father...
> because I said, 'I am God's Son'? I am the one God chose and sent into the world. If I don't do what my Father does, then don't believe me. But if I do what my Father does, even though you don't believe in me, believe what I do. Then you will know and understand that the Father is in me and I am in the Father. (ncv)

learned in earlier chapters, the gospel of Jesus Christ is much more than simply "fire insurance" or a "ticket to heaven" to be cashed in when we die. It concerns our life-style in this present world; that is, how we relate to others in our everyday life situations. It was this relationship issue that moved Jesus to speak words of comfort to His worried disciples in the upper room. As He encouraged them, He was unveiling the very heart of

Family Identity

Alpha Series
Abiding In Christ

Salvation through faith
- (Security) From the penalty of sin
- (Significance) From the power and dominion of sin

The promise
John 14:19-20

Yet a little while, and the world seeth me no more; but ye see me: because I live, ye shall live also. At that day ye shall know that I am in my Father, and ye in me, and I in you. (kjv)

Abiding
Jesus . . . . . the vine
Disciples. . . the branches
Father. . . . . the vinegrower

the gospel: to trust in Himself, and do His works. When Jesus promised them another Comforter, He was assuring them that He would come and live with them, and together they would be one in the Spirit. He summarized all He was saying by that fantastic promise of John 14:20 in which we are assured that just as He is in the Father, we are in Him, and He is in us.

To help us understand the practical meaning of this union with Christ, Jesus gave His disciples an analogy of the grapevine, and it's branches, (John 15:1-8). In this analogy, He equates Himself to the vine, His disciples to the branches, and the Father as the vinegrower or gardener. Our union with Jesus is depicted as the branch and the vine being inseparably joined so that all we are and all we produce is based on this vital union. Just as the branches draw their nourishment and strength to bear fruit from the vine, so also believers receive their personal security and significance from Christ in order to love others (bear fruit). Just as the gardener prunes the branches to cause them to bear more fruit, so also the Father directs and disciplines His own children to produce the "peaceable fruit of righteousness" in their lives, (Hebrews 12).

Practical Abiding

Although the analogy of the vine is a very beautiful picture of our union with Christ, its main point is to direct our attention to what Jesus meant when He said, "Abide in me, and I in you," (verse 4). This analogy answers the questions many Christians are asking.

First, the term "abide" simply means to "live" or "dwell." It is not as much concerned with specific actions as it is with a life-style in general. As the bird "abides" in the air or the fish "abides" in the sea, we are called upon to abide in Christ.

Second, it is a life-style based upon our being "in Christ Jesus," therefore, considering what we studied earlier, we can conclude it is a operating life-style of grace rather than a functioning life-style of law.

Alpha Series
Abiding In Christ

Third, *A grace life-style is motivated by faith, hope, and love rather than fear, guilt, and pride.*

Fourth, to abide in Christ means we are living out the gospel in the power of the Holy Spirit (rather than in our own power) on a daily basis. *Not to abide in Christ is to live on the basis of our power to do good.*

To help us understand what it means to live out the gospel on a daily basis, we need to learn how to do "the trip in." This means we simply examine ourselves in everyday situations on several different levels to determine what is going on inside at any given moment. The table below illustrates the levels we need to examine honestly.

Rather than simply looking at our situations, and complaining about them, we must learn to look *inside ourselves* if we are

The vine and the branches  John 15:1-8

1. *I am the true vine, and my Father is the vine-grower.*
2. *He removes every branch in me that bears no fruit. Every branch that bears fruit he prunes to make it bear more fruit.*
3. *You have already been cleansed by the word that I have spoken to you.*
4. *Abide in me as I abide in you. Just as the branch cannot bear fruit by itself unless it abides in the vine, neither can you unless you abide in me.*
5. *I am the vine, you are the branches. Those who abide in me and I in them bear much fruit, because apart from me you can do nothing.*
6. *Whoever does not abide in me is thrown away like a branch and withers; such branches are gathered, thrown into the fire, and burned.*
7. *If you abide in me, and my words abide in you, ask for whatever you wish, and it will be done for you.*
8. *My Father is glorified by this, that you bear much fruit and become my disciples.* (ncv)

going to abide in Christ. We must honestly examine our own behavior, emotions, and beliefs in spite of the temptation to judge and criticize others in that situation. When we do, *we will soon discover the natural responses of the flesh that need to be brought into the light of our own awareness, and confessed before God.*

Based on the various false assumptions concerning our worth as persons, we will be plagued with a sense of guilt that leads us to self-protective manipulation out of a heart of pride. Remember, there is nothing pretty about that sin nature we call the flesh. The willingness to explore our own inward motivations is a big part of what John called "walking in the light, as He is in the light," (1 John 1:7). It means that we are honest enough with God and ourselves to recognize the works of our own flesh while trusting in our

Alpha Series
Abiding In Christ

position as new persons in Christ. The promise for doing so is intimacy with God through cleansing from the power of sin otherwise known as abiding in Christ.

> ➤ Just exactly what does it mean to abide in Christ and He in us?
> ➤ How do we know we are abiding in Him?
> ➤ What "fruit" will we bear if we abide in Him?

1. To abide in means to live in or dwell in
2. Abiding is a lifestyle of grace; not a lifestyle of law
3. Abiding is motivated by faith, hope and love; not fear guilt and pride
4. We live the gospel in the power of the holy spirit, not our own power

THE TRIP INSIDE

For This Situation:	CONFESS This Motivation:	Produces this Manipulation	BELIEVE This Motivation	Produces this Ministry
Behavior	Pride	Works of the Flesh	Love	Fruit of the Spirit
Feelings	Guilt	Hate/Self-pity/Anxiety	Hope	Love/Joy/Peace
Thoughts	Fear	"I will be worthy if . . ."	Faith	"I am worthy because"

Bearing Fruit

The promise Jesus gives to those who abide in Him is summarized by the concept of bearing fruit. When we are willing to confess our false assumptions, and how they produce the sinful emotions which lead to the works of the flesh in our daily lives, the Father cleanses us from the inside out. Such cleansing or pruning is necessary to replace the false assumptions with Biblical truth that will work itself out, through faith, in hope and love for others. Since all we do or say must be motivated by divine love if it is

Alpha Series
Abiding In Christ

Abiding Motivations

REPLACE

WITH

to be of any value as ministry rather than manipulation, we cannot "bear fruit" unless the fear, guilt, and pride of the flesh is replaced by the faith, hope, and love of the Spirit. *True fruit bearing requires the work of the Holy Spirit producing in us the love, joy, peace, longsuffering, gentleness, goodness, faith, meekness, and temperance necessary to display the character of Christ.* Bearing fruit is not a flurry of religious activities motivated out of the flesh, but rather the *consistent display of the character of Christ in our everyday lives*. It is not simply a religious duty to be performed, but a life-style of grace. Bearing fruit is characterized by keeping your eyes on the grace of God as expressed in Jesus, and not on what you are doing or what is being done to you. Self-evaluation should always be done on the basis of your motivation (see the previous table), not on the basis of your performance. Hope and love based on faith are the motivations to look for. If you find fear, guilt, and pride in any given circumstance, you have forgotten the grace of God and who you are (2 Peter 1:9).

    A failure to abide in Christ not only hinders the production of fruit by the branch, but also is harmful to the branch itself. Jesus warned that not abiding in Him caused a branch to be "cast forth," and "withered." Furthermore, He says that men gather the "withered branches," and burn them. It is important to note that He is not talking about being sent to hell, but is referring to the interpersonal strife and relational dysfunction that naturally comes from operating on false assumptions, and engaging in a variety of manipulation

Alpha Series
Abiding In Christ

tactics. A failure to abide in Christ makes us susceptible to all the relational turmoil and dysfunction of the rest of the world.

In contrast to such personal and relational death, however, Jesus promises that those who abide in Him "will ask what ye will, and it shall be done unto you." This means that when we are abiding in Christ, and His words abide in us, (i.e. we are operating on Biblical assumptions of our worth), that we are able to experience effective communication with the Father. As we become aware of our oneness with Jesus and the Father, we are able to flow in His plan for our lives and reveal His character in our daily walk. *When we manifest the character of Christ in our homes, on the job, or in our communities, we actually glorify the Father.* What Jesus had in mind from the very beginning was that all His disciples would love one another by the fruit of the Spirit so that His Father would be glorified. Thus, He calls on us to abide in Him by faith in what He says He has already done for us.

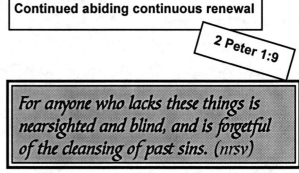

Continued abiding continuous renewal

2 Peter 1:9

For anyone who lacks these things is nearsighted and blind, and is forgetful of the cleansing of past sins. (nrsv)

Alpha Series
Abiding In Christ

QUESTIONS

CHAPTER ELEVEN: ABIDING IN CHRIST

Lesson One: The Vine and the Branches

1. Based upon Jesus' own testimony, what was the key to His miraculous life and ministry as the Son of Man?

2. What has been our main purpose in this study?

3. Based upon John 14:19-20, what was the basis of the assurance Jesus was providing?

4. What is the significance of the grapevine analogy given in John 15:1-8?

5. What is abiding in Christ all about?

6. What is abiding motivation?

7. If you find you lack these motivations what is the cause? See 1 Peter 1:9.

Alpha Series
Abiding In Christ

ABIDING IN CHRIST — Chapter 11
LIVING IN CHRIST'S LOVE — Lesson 2

Closely associated with the privilege of abiding in Christ, is the call of Jesus to continue in His love. There can be NO greater sense of personal satisfaction than that which comes from continually living in the love of Jesus Christ. For that reason Jesus encouraged His worried disciples by calling them to live out their lives within the context of His divine love. We can experience personal satisfaction and relational health only when we learn to live daily in the love of Jesus.

The Father's Love

To help His nervous disciples understand the call to live in His love, Jesus used His own relationship with the Father as an example. *"As the Father hath loved me, so have I loved you: continue ye in my love. If ye keep my commandments, ye shall abide in my love; even as I have kept my Father's commandments, and abide in His love"*, *(John 15:9-10)*. In exactly the same way that God the Father loved His only begotten Son, Jesus, all of Christ's disciples are loved by Jesus. His love is, therefore, that kind of divine love that is unconditional, sacrificial, eternal, initiating, and intelligent. It is not to be compared with human love that can never truly meet our needs for security, but is far superior in all respects. The call to continue or abide in that divine love of Christ is really a call to continually base our personal security on the love that Jesus has for us.

The love of the Father for Jesus is taken for granted and never questioned. No one thinks perhaps the Father did not love Jesus. No one thinks, perhaps the Father was even *able* to hate Jesus; or that somehow the Father had a choice, he could either love Jesus or not love Jesus. The Father loved Jesus because love is the nature of the Father. Loving is an unconditional and unchangeable aspect of his nature. God is love! To love is the way he is, —he cannot be otherwise.

This is also true when applied to us. Remember, everything true of Jesus is true of us as well. God's love for us is absolutely dependable. This is the basis for all we believe.

> **John 15 9-10**
>
> **The nature of Jesus' love**
>
> As the Father hath loved me, so have I loved you: continue ye in my love. If ye keep my commandments, ye shall abide in my love; even as I have kept my Father's commandments, and abide in His love. (kjv)

God's love is:
- Unconditional
- Sacrificial
- Eternal
- Initiating
- Intelligent

Alpha Series
Abiding in Christ

God's love for us is as dependable as is God being God. Somehow many have come to believe God's love for them depends on their behavior... that God loves some more than others... that if he chooses to do so, he can stop loving them, especially if they do not behave themselves.

However, the truth, revealed in scripture, is that such thinking is untrue. God's love for us is as permanent as God is permanent. God's love for us is as unchangeable as God is unchangeable. The only way for God to not love us or change his love for us is for God to stop being God! This he cannot do. The proof of this is the cross (John 3:16). His love compelled him to send Jesus to suffer, and die for us. Such is his love. It is absolutely dependable. He will do everything it takes to assure everyone of salvation. Jesus' sacrifice was everything. God did not stop at anything, even the sacrifice of his own son Jesus. God did what it took; this was his love. This love is ours.

> *God never stops loving us, regardless*

To help us understand how we are to abide in His love, Jesus tells us that obedience to His commands is the key to abiding in His love just as He was always abiding in God's love by obeying His Father's commands. At first glance we may think that Jesus is saying if we keep His command He will love us but if we do not keep His commands He will not love us. Nothing could be farther from the truth since His love is equated with the Father's love which is *unconditional* in nature, and not dependant upon our conduct in any way. Instead, Jesus is defining what His love looks like so we might know how to live in it continually. He defines His love in action. Just as the Father's love was revealed by His commands to Jesus, the love of Christ is revealed to us by His commands to us. This kind of love is exemplified in the Garden of Gethsemane, where Jesus declares His willingness to suffer and die rather than to disobey His Father's will.

> *God's commandments, his will, describe his love in action.*

Like the Father's love for His Son, Jesus' love for us is so intimate and personal that He is concerned about every detail of our lives. His commands are not to be viewed as a set of dreadful obligations or duties that we must complete in order to obtain His favor and blessing; but rather His personal, loving direction in our lives so we may be secure in all we do or experience. To keep His commandments, then, is to abide in His love because His love and His commandments are one and the same. His commandments describe what love looks like in action. Jesus loves us so much that He is always leading us into the best possible life at any given time. If we are going to abide in His love, then, we will be keeping His commandments; that is, doing the activity of love. Just as Jesus could count on the Father loving Him and expressing His love

> *God's love for us is never dependent upon what we do for him.*

Alpha Series
Abiding in Christ

through personal direction each day, so we may count on Jesus expressing His love for us in His personal commands to us each day.

The Promise of Joy

The ultimate purpose for both the analogy of the vine and the call to abide in His love is explained by Jesus in John 15:11. "These things have I spoken unto you, that my joy might remain in you, and that your joy might be full." The specific "things" Jesus spoke of are the call to (1) abide in Him, (2) continue in His love, and (3) keep His commands. The personal reason He gives for us to heed "these things" is that His joy might remain in us, and that our joy might be full.

It was for "the joy that was set before Him" that Jesus was able to "endure the cross", (Hebrews 12:2). And it is that same joy that causes us to "rejoice with joy unspeakable, and full of glory" (1 Peter 1:9), in spite of the trials of life. As used in this context, the term "joy" refers to that inward state of contentment and personal satisfaction that comes from the Holy Spirit when we abide in Christ, continue in His love,

> *Joy is not a goal*

and keep His commandments. This promise of joy needs to be understood by every believer as the by-product of our ministry, and not the ultimate end in itself. That is, *the experience of joy cannot be obtained by making it our ultimate goal*, but rather by abiding in Christ, continuing in His love, and keeping His commands.

It may be useful at this point to remind ourselves that God has not chosen to leave us in this sin cursed world in sin cursed bodies so that we may feel good. Instead, He has left us here to represent His Son Jesus as "ambassadors," and complete the work that Jesus began. The promise of joy, then, is not to be understood as a promise that all will go well with us in this world, but rather a promise of satisfaction that comes from living out daily who God has made us to be in Christ. It is the personal satisfaction that we may enjoy when we

> **Joy**
> *The by-product of our ministry and not the ultimate end in itself*

Living in Christ's Love

Alpha Series
Abiding in Christ

are used of God by the power of His Spirit to minister to the needs of others around us.

Ministry or Manipulation?

Continuing in John 15, in verses 12 and 13, Jesus brought His disciples (and us) back to the original point of this discourse. *"This is my commandment, that ye love one another, as I have loved you. Greater love hath no man than this, that a man lay down his life for his friends."* What Jesus wanted us to understand, from the analogy of the vine, and the call to abide in His love, was that He has left us here to love one another in His absence. He defines divine love as the kind that will lay down its own life for the welfare of others, not only in a literal physical death but also in living for others before oneself. He would soon reveal this kind of unselfish love during the last hours of His earthly ministry. He would submit Himself to the agony of the garden, the humiliation of His arrest and trial, and the shameful death on the cross for the sake of others. It is to that same kind of love that He is calling all His disciples. Only as we abide in Christ, continue in His love, and keep His commandments can we truly love one another enough to lay down our lives in life or death. Otherwise, our relationships with others may appear to be loving (on the surface) but, in reality, be self-serving, and religious manipulation.

> **Ministry or manipulation?**
> The basic difference between ministry and manipulation is not revealed in our actions, but rather our motives.

> **Manipulation**
>
> **Apperent Joy**
> - **FEAR** — Abiding in yourself
> - **GUILT** — Trying to makeup
> - **PRIDE** — Demonstration for self gain

> **Apparent or real?**

It is important to note the difference between the true ministry of divine love Jesus is calling us to, and the religious manipulation that often takes its place. The basic difference between ministry and manipulation is not revealed in our actions, but rather our motives. To love others as Christ means we are motivated by faith, (abiding in Christ), hope, (continuing in His love for us), and love, (keeping His commands to love). When our motives are

Alpha Series
Abiding in Christ

faith, hope, and love we will minister effectively in our relationships with others.

In contrast to the motives of grace, however, we are naturally driven by fear, guilt, and pride. These are the motives of the flesh which always drive us to manipulate rather than minister. Since we yet live in a physical body with the sinful nature of the flesh, we must always contend with its motives. By confessing our fear, guilt, and pride of the flesh, we can experience the forgiveness and cleansing necessary to purify our motives. As the psalmist, David, prays in Psalm 51:10-12, "Create in me a clean heart, O God, and renew a right spirit within me. Cast me not away from Your presence, and take not Your Holy Spirit from me. Restore to me the joy of Your salvation, and uphold me *with* a willing spirit."

In order to truly love others as Christ, (i.e. minister to rather than manipulate others), we must be willing to have the Spirit of God search our hearts to expose and cleanse the false motives. As He cleanses us from our natural fear of failure and rejection, He replaces it with the faith we need to abide in Christ. As He sweeps away our natural guilt and sense of condemnation, He fills us with the hope we need to continue in the love of Christ. As He purges us of fleshly pride, He floods our hearts with the love of God so that we keep the commands of Christ to love others as He did.

The way to recognize whether or not we are truly ministering the love of Christ to others is to honestly examine our motives—not by looking at their response to our ministry. Jesus revealed these things so His joy might remain in us, and our joy might be full. When we are abiding in Christ by faith, continuing in His love with hope, and keeping His commands to love, we are satisfied, and content *regardless of the response of others*. This kind of ministry is its own reward. It is certainly nice, and feels good when others respond to us favorably, but it is not necessary. Because of the comfort of the Spirit we receive personally, we may continue to minister rather than manipulate no matter what the response of others may be.

Alpha Series
Abiding in Christ

QUESTIONS

CHAPTER ELEVEN: ABIDING IN CHRIST

Lesson Two: Living In Christ's Love

1. To help us understand the call to live in love what key concept did Jesus give us? See John 15:9-10.

2. What are the five characteristics of God's love?

3. Why is the love of God for us so certain?

4. Based on our performance records, why is God's kind of love so important to us?

5. What characterizes true ministry and joy?

6. What characterizes false ministry or manipulation?

7. What does it take to truly love others as Christ?

THE OVERCOMER — Chapter 12
THE MINISTRY OF THE OVERCOMER — Lesson 1

The Bible has a very special term for those who are believers in Jesus Christ and are abiding in Him. They are referred to as "overcomers" to emphasize their victory over the spiritual enemies of the flesh, the world system, and Satan. Although Jesus promised His disciples that they would encounter extreme opposition from the world, He assured them that He had overcome the world. By virtue of our union with Christ, we who are in Christ, and have Christ abiding in us, are also overcomers; "For whatsoever is born of God overcometh the world... Who is he that overcometh the world, but he that believeth that Jesus is the Son of God?"

In this lesson we shall examine the specific ways we as overcomers, as victors, as conquerors, as winners are going to minister to others. All that we have learned concerning the gospel of Jesus Christ is what allows us to experience personal victory as overcomers. It is time to help others be overcomers as well; to follow through with our real purpose in being used by God. The fact that all believers are called of God to minister to the needs of others is repeatedly emphasized in the various "one another" passages of the New Testament.

The instruction given by the

1 John 5:4-5

The overcomer

4 For whatsoever is born of God overcometh the world...
5 Who is he that overcometh the world, but he that believeth that Jesus is the Son of God? (kjv)

The conqueror

4 For whatever is born of God conquers the world...
5 Who is it that conquers the world but the one who believes that Jesus is the Son of God? (nrsv)

The winner

4 Because everyone who is a child of God conquers the world. And this is the victory that conquers the world—our faith.
5 So the one who wins against the world is the person who believes that Jesus is the Son of God. (ncv)

apostle Paul in 1 Thessalonians 5:14 provides us with a working outline for the relational ministry of all overcomers. After admonishing the church to comfort and edify one another, (verse 11), Paul directs the "brethren", (brothers and sisters in Christ), to recognize and respect the spiritual leadership within their church. It is important to note that the church leaders were to be known *by their labor* as opposed to their educational status or religious title. Likewise, they were to be loved and respected *because of their relational ministries rather than political position* within the organization. Such recognition of *true* church leadership would minimize the fleshly tendency toward interpersonal strife, jealousy, and divisions so common in today's churches.

> **2 Corinthians 13:5**
>
> *Examine yourselves to see whether you are living in the faith. Test yourselves. Do you not realize that Jesus Christ is in you?—Unless, indeed, you fail to meet the test!* (ncv)

As part of the recognition of spiritual leadership, it was also necessary for the brethren to realize that their leaders were "set before them by means of the Lord" *to equip them for the work of the ministry*. Before the third century, there was no distinction between the clergy, (paid professionals), and the laity in the church. *The ministry was not the responsibility of a professional clergyman, but was the duty of all believers.* True leaders saw their task as equipping the saints, (all believers), to do the work of the ministry so the body of Christ would be edified, (see Ephesians 4:11-16). For this reason Paul goes on to beseech the <u>brethren</u>, the saints of God, believers in Jesus Christ, to carry out their relational ministry in the church.

> Leaders were known for their labor and relational ministries as opposed to their educational status, religious title or political position. Their job was to equip the body for the work of the ministry.

Warn the Unruly

The first level of relational ministry overcomers are called to is confrontational in nature. The phrase, "warn them that are unruly" refers to the job of confronting those who are behaving inappropriately. The idea here is to love another enough to get involved with them when we see them doing or saying things that may harm themselves or others. The word translated "warn" in the King James Version comes from a Greek word which literally means "to put in mind" implying that we are to challenge faulty belief systems, and attitudes.

Keep in mind who it is to be warning the unruly. *He does not beseech pastors or professional counselors*, but rather the brethren to warn those who are unruly. Even though

Alpha Series
The Overcomer

it is far easier in the flesh to simply report the unruly to the church leaders and insist that they warn them, the command is for the brethren to do the confronting. The same thought is expressed in Galatians 6:1, "Brethren, if a man be overtaken in a fault, ye which are spiritual, restore such a one in the spirit of meekness; considering thyself, lest thou also be tempted." Again the command to confront and restore is not given to paid professionals, but to those brethren who are spiritual, that is those controlled by the Holy Spirit.

> Galatians 6:1
>
> *Brethren, if a man be overtaken in a fault, ye which are spiritual, restore such a one in the spirit of meekness; considering thyself, lest thou also be tempted* (kjv)

The warning of this last verse is important for all of us to understand. When we set about to confront and restore one who is "unruly" or "overtaken in a fault", *we must also consider ourselves very carefully*. That is, *we must examine our own motivation* to be sure it is of the Spirit rather than the flesh so we may warn and restore out of a pure heart of love and not pride. In confronting those who are behaving inappropriately we also may be tempted to judge them rather than love them. By confessing our own fleshly motivations of the flesh, (fear, guilt, and pride), we receive the forgiveness and cleansing we need to be motivated by faith, hope, and love. We get the "beam out of our own eye before we try to remove the splinter from our brother's eye". Remember, the difference between ministry and manipulation is motive.

> **Three levels of relational ministry**
> 1. Warn the unruly (confrontational)
> 2. Comfort the emotionally distraught
> 3. Support the weak in faith

Comfort the Feebleminded

The second level of our relational ministry as overcomers has to do with giving comfort to those who are "feebleminded" or emotionally distraught. We are not simply to concern ourselves with the brother's behavior, but also with his emotional state. To be used of God to bring comfort to those who are hurting emotionally is certainly one of the most needful ministries in our communities today. Those around us who are struggling with personal issues, financial problems, family crisis, etc., and are *in desperate need of people who understand, and care about their feelings*. They do not need great theological answers as much as they need a handshake, a warm smile, or a friendly hug. Simply being present with those who are suffering emotionally offers a great deal more comfort than eloquent speeches and philosophies of men.

Alpha Series
The Overcomer

In II Corinthians 1:3-4 we are told, "Blessed be . . . the God of all comfort; who comforteth us in all our tribulation, *that we may be able to comfort them which are in any trouble,* by the comfort wherewith we ourselves are comforted of God." The comfort that overcomers have to offer others is that which they have received from God by believing the gospel in the middle of their own trials. Although much more could be said about the role we play in comforting one another, it is enough for now to understand that it is not what you say that counts as much as simply being present to listen to, weep with, and endure the personal pain others are enduring. Your being there says, "I love you," and brings comfort to those who are hurting like nothing else can do.

Support the Weak

The final level of our relational ministry involves the personal support of those who are weak in the faith. *These folks have trouble believing the gospel for themselves.* They rarely think of what God has done in Christ to make them personally secure or significant, and are usually busy trying to "prove themselves" worthy in their own eyes. As a result the weak brother tends to be both religious and obnoxious at the same time. He is usually very legalistic in his thinking, and is likely to criticize others, and condemn himself. Our natural reaction to such a brother is to avoid him at all costs.

In Romans 14:1, Paul instructs the overcomer, (one who is strong in the faith), to receive rather than avoid the weak brother. This means that we are to become personally involved in supporting those who are weak in the faith, and not trouble them about their "doubtful issues". The "doubtful issues" are simply those things in our lives that the Bible does not directly address. However, the weak brother will feel obligated to make up a list of rules about such matters, and impose them on himself and others. The difficult part of supporting the weak brother is in accepting him in spite of his critical spirit, and often obnoxious behavior.

The way we truly support the weak brother is to see him through the eyes of our

> **Romans 14:1**
> *Welcome those who are weak in faith, but not for the purpose of quarreling over opinions.* (nrsv)

> To truly support him, we must believe the gospel for the weak brother

Alpha Series
The Overcomer

Savior. The weak brother is generally motivated by fear, guilt, and pride, therefore, he presents a fairly tough religious shell that is meant to protect him from further hurt. Further, he manipulates others to make himself look good. The overcomer must learn to look past the religious facades of the weak brother to see a worthy but frightened child of God.

To truly support him, we must believe the gospel for the weak brother. Sooner or later his religious facades will crack and crumble, and he will desperately need to hear again the good news that he is secure only in God's unconditional love, and significant only in God's sovereign plan.

The weak in faith

- Fix-it people
- Legalistic people
- They walk by sight
- Judge the behavior of others
- They love to tell others what to do
- Quick to spout rules and regulations
- They love to be seen doing good deeds
- They think in terms of right and wrong
- Are thinking about how they look to others
- They are motivated by fear, guilt and pride
- They seek to please God by their activities
- What they do is important, not their faith
- They think and talk in terms of shoulds and oughts
- They think in terms of receiving curses for bad deeds
- They operate on the basis of principles rather than love
- They think in terms of receiving blessings for good deeds

It is by means of the relational ministry that we overcome the spiritual opposition against the gospel of Jesus Christ. As we warn the unruly, comfort the feebleminded, and support the weak, we are keeping the commands of Jesus to love one another in the same manner that He loves us. As we believe the gospel for ourselves, and are set free to believe the gospel for others, we declare to the world that we are truly overcomers.

Alpha Series
The Overcomer

QUESTIONS

CHAPTER TWELVE: THE OVERCOMER

Lesson One: The Ministry of the Overcomer

1. What is the key to overcoming the world—and is our victory? See 1 John 5:4-5.

2. According to 1 Thessalonians 5:14, who is to warn the unruly?

3. Why are we admonished to consider ourselves when warning the unruly?

4. Who is responsible for the ministry of the church?

5. Who are the feebleminded or the fainthearted?

6. Based upon II Corinthians 1:3-4, what is the basis of our comforting others?

7. Who are the weak? See Romans 14:1.

8. What is the basis for our supporting the weak of faith?

THE OVERCOMER
THE OVERCOMER'S CHURCH
Chapter 12, Lesson 2

The concept of relational ministry can not be fully understood apart from the Biblical idea of the church. Throughout His public ministry, Jesus was training a small group of men He called to be apostles, or the foundational structure of the church. After His resurrection He met with these men again in the upper room to commission them to the ministry of the gospel. For the next 40 days He encouraged them with at least a half dozen personal appearances. In each recorded appearance, Jesus promised His disciples He would provide the power and direction they needed to begin to function as the church He himself had promised to build. In this closing study we will examine the nature and mission of the overcomer's church.

The Revelation of the Church

The first mention of the church in the Bible is recorded in Matthew 16:13-19. It was during a retreat at a resort called Caesarea Philippi that Jesus began to reveal the idea of the church to His disciples. They had been with Him for several years, and were resting from His public ministry when Jesus asked them who people thought He was, (verse 13). While He certainly knew who He was, Jesus was concerned with how His dis-

> **Matthew 16:13-19**
>
> 13 When Jesus came to the area of Caesarea Philippi, he asked his followers, "Who do people say the Son of Man is?"
> 14 They answered, "Some say you are John the Baptist. Others say you are Elijah, and still others say you are Jeremiah or one of the prophets."
> 15 Then Jesus asked them, "And who do you say I am?"
> 16 Simon Peter answered, "You are the Christ, the Son of the living God."
> 17 Jesus answered, "You are blessed, Simon son of Jonah, because no person taught you that. My Father in heaven showed you who I am.
> 18 So I tell you, you are Peter. On this rock I will build my church, and the power of death (gates of Hades-nrsv) will not be able to defeat it.
> 19 I will give you the keys of the kingdom of heaven; the things you don't allow on earth will be the things that God does not allow, and the things you allow on earth will be the things that God allows." (ncv)

ciples were going to face the hostile public opinion as He went to Jerusalem to be rejected and crucified. So He asked His disciples what they had heard about Him.

Trying to be as optimistic as possible, the disciples reported some thought He was John the Baptist come back from the dead, some thought He was the prophet Elijah or Jeremiah. Not one reported people thought He was who He claimed to be—no one believed He was really the Messiah.

Knowing His disciples were troubled by this negative public opinion of Himself, Jesus pressed them further by asking what they thought about His true identity. Simon Peter identified Jesus as "the Christ, the Son of the living God," and Jesus replied he was blessed because human reasoning and intellect had not led him to this conclusion, but the personal revelation of God the Father. Jesus' response indicates a cardinal principle for the church to remember. *Only by a personal revelation of God can we truly recognize who Jesus really is.*

> **Cardinal principles of revelation**
> - *Only by a personal revelation of God can we truly recognize who Jesus really is.*
> - *So also is divine revelation necessary to recognize the true nature of the church.*

In connection with the revelation of His true identity, Jesus went on to speak of the church. Similarly, Jesus' response indicates another cardinal principle for the church to remember. *Just as divine revelation is required to recognize who Jesus is, so also is divine revelation necessary to recognize the true nature of the church.* Human wisdom and reasoning will not recognize the church as anything other than a religious organization or club. But the scriptures reveal it is *an organism, not an organization*, the body of Christ, which continually expresses the life and character of Jesus in this world today. The church is the body of Christ in the world. It acts as his physical presence, each member personally led by his Spirit. While the physical body of Jesus is with His father in heaven, the church becomes His physical representation to the world. It is through the church, His body, that He acts.

> *The church is an organism, not an organization.*

> *It is through the church, His body, Jesus acts in the world.*

The Foundation of the Church

The term "church" is derived from a compound Greek word, "ecclesia," which literally means a called out assembly or group. When Jesus

> **Ecclesia**
> *Called out assembly or group*

Alpha Series
The Overcomer

Entry into the ecclesia

> And who do you say I am?

said He would build His "church," He was saying that He would call out, and assemble a group. The play on words He used concerning Peter's name ("petros" meaning stone), and the rock ("petra" meaning massive rock formation) was intended by Jesus

The real foundation

Petros = stone = Peter
Petra = rock = Jesus

Come to the Living Stone *1 Peter 2:4-12*

⁴ Come to the Lord Jesus, the "stone" that lives. The people of the world did not want this stone, but he was the stone God chose, and he was precious.

⁵ You also are like living stones, so let yourselves be used to build a spiritual temple--to be holy priests who offer spiritual sacrifices to God. He will accept those sacrifices through Jesus Christ.

⁶ The Scripture says: "I will put a stone in the ground in Jerusalem. Everything will be built on this important and precious rock. Anyone who trusts in him will never be disappointed."

⁷ This stone is worth much to you who believe. But to the people who do not believe, "the stone that the builders rejected has become the cornerstone."

⁸ Also, he is "a stone that causes people to stumble, a rock that makes them fall." They stumble because they do not obey what God says, which is what God planned to happen to them.

⁹ But you are a chosen people, royal priests, a holy nation, a people for God's own possession. You were chosen to tell about the wonderful acts of God, who called you out of darkness into his wonderful light.

¹⁰ At one time you were not a people, but now you are God's people. In the past you had never received mercy, but now you have received God's mercy.

¹¹ Dear friends, you are like foreigners and strangers in this world. I beg you to avoid the evil things your bodies want to do that fight against your soul.

¹² People who do not believe are living all around you and might say that you are doing wrong. Live such good lives that they will see the good things you do and will give glory to God on the day when Christ comes again. *(ncv)*

to teach us His church was not going to be founded upon a man, (like so many cults), but was to be built upon Himself as the "Rock of Ages." The foundation for the church that Jesus is building is not human effort or planning, but divine power and wisdom. The people who constitute the church that Jesus builds are those who are joined to Him personally, and joined by Him to each other. They are brought into relationship with one another by divine appointment to be the body of Christ.

Jesus, Himself, is the builder of the church as well as the foundation of the church therefore there is no need to become ensnared by the religious games and politics we have witnessed throughout church history. Our goals can remain relational in nature rather than set on establishing religious programs of various sorts. We can have less "do do" and more ministry. If Jesus is truly recognized as both the foundation, and builder of the church, then we need not devote our lives to building church edifices, establishing church programs, and raising funds to make them "successful." Instead, we can devote ourselves to relationships—believing the gospel for ourselves and for each other in our homes, on our jobs, and in our communities.

The Mission and Purpose of the Church

Jesus promised that the gates of hell would not prevail against the church He builds. A proper understanding of that promise requires a radically dif-ferent view of the mission and purpose of the church than has been commonly held. Rather than being a large fortress in which we might seek refuge from the attack of Satan, the church was designed to be a spiritual army that literally smashes through the "gates" or defenses of hell itself. The idea of this promise is Satan, and all the forces of hell itself, cannot withstand the power of the church to set the captives free. The church, the ecclesia, is meant to be offensive in nature not defensive. The church is meant to be moving out into the world sharing the gospel through relationships, not retreating and defensive.

Matthew 16:18

> *So I tell you, you are Peter. On this rock I will build my church, and the power of death (gates of Hades-nrsv) will not be able to defeat it. (ncv)*

To fully appreciate this promise of power, we must recognize that *the church Jesus builds is not contained in a building, or restricted to a one hour program on Sunday morning.* If our concept of the church is narrowed down to a religious gathering of people in a religious building for a religious program of singing and preaching on Sunday morning, then we have missed the entire point of this promise. We need to broaden our vision of the church to include the gathering of two or three in the name of (fully identifying themselves with) Jesus. This means that *"church" can happen more at home, on the job, or in the community than it does in a special building on Sunday morning.*

The purpose Jesus has in mind for calling out a group of two or three—or a group of two or three thousand, is *to live out the gospel in relationships*. By this we mean when we relate to other people we are believing the gospel for ourselves and others regardless of what the circumstances may be. The relational ministry Jesus has called each of us to is to be lived constantly in our normal, walking around, every day lives. It is not limited to a Sunday morning worship service. Believers <u>are</u> the church,, and the gospel they believe and share is the "power of God unto salvation,": therefore, the church Jesus builds is *continually* meeting and fulfilling its mission by sharing the gospel in our daily relationships. As we continually meet and share the gospel Jesus promises the defenses of hell itself cannot withstand the power of that gospel.

> The purpose Jesus has for the ecclesia is to live out the gospel in relationships.

The Authority of the Church

To complete His revelation of the church Jesus promised that He would give them the "keys of the kingdom of heaven." His church would have the authority to represent Jesus in the world. Literally, He promised, "whatever you decide at one point in time on earth shall have already been decided and continue to be decided in heaven." This simply means the church would express, not determine, what Jesus had decided in heaven. As the divine Head, Jesus has absolute authority over the church which is called the "body of Christ." He makes the decisions concerning it's ministry in heaven and the body has His authority to express that decision on earth. The authority to express the will of Christ in the world is the wonderful privilege of "being Christ" to the world about us.

The purpose of the church is to carry on the works of Christ. There are many other things that could be said about the overcomer's church, and its divine authority to express the will of Christ. However, the main point is Jesus came, not to be ministered to, but to minister; to seek and to save that which was lost. It is the purpose of the church to express that character, and that mission of Jesus in this world. The church is to be Christ in the world. Apart from the church, Christ will not be represented.

The significance of the believer is related to being part of the body of Christ. As part of his body, those who represent him in the world, his ambassadors, the believer is called to be Christ to those around him; to be Christ to others, to spread the message of reconciliation. We are not called to be a part of the world but, to be a part of His world, the church. Apart from those acting as the true body, Christ will not be represented in the world. He has chosen how His gospel will be delivered—by Him, through His physical representa-

Alpha Series
The Overcomer

2 Cor 5:17-6:2 — **The ministry of reconciliation**

> *17 So if anyone is in Christ, there is a new creation: everything old has passed away; see, everything has become new!*
> *18 All this is from God, who reconciled us to himself through Christ, and has given us the ministry of reconciliation;*
> *19 that is, in Christ God was reconciling the world to himself, not counting their trespasses against them, and entrusting the message of reconciliation to us.*
> *20 So we are ambassadors for Christ, since God is making his appeal through us; we entreat you on behalf of Christ, be reconciled to God.*
> *21 For our sake he made him to be sin who knew no sin, so that in him we might become the righteousness of God.*
> *6:1 As we work together with him, we urge you also not to accept the grace of God in vain.*
> *2 For he says, "At an acceptable time I have listened to you, and on a day of salvation I have helped you. See, now is the acceptable time; see, now is the day of salvation."*

tion in the world—the church. It is the church that will spread the message of reconciliation and love. He will lead the church in the hearts of the members, through His Spirit. To that end He has promised that He would give us the supernatural power we need to be Christ to each other and the world about us. May God grant us the grace to begin at home with our own families, and reach out to those around us on a daily basis.

The keys — **Matthew 16:19**

> *I will give you the keys of the kingdom of heaven; the things you don't allow on earth will be the things that God does not allow, and the things you allow on earth will be the things that God allows. (ncv)*

Alpha Series
The Overcomer

QUESTIONS

CHAPTER TWELVE: THE OVERCOMER

Lesson Two: The Overcomer's Church

1. What is the church?

2. How does Jesus act in the world?

3. Who is the foundation of the church?

4. What is the mission of the church?

5. In speaking about the authority of the church—the keys, what is Jesus talking about in Matthew 16:19?

6. What is the main purpose of the church?

APPENDIX

ALPHA STUDY GUIDE BIBLE REFERENCES

LESSON 1.1 Who Are You?
God formed man and   **GENESIS**
  man became a living being. --- 2:7
                                                                                                JOHN
Jesus knew what was in man. ---2:25

LESSON 1.2 Family Identity   **GENESIS**
It was not good for man to be alone ---2:18
God caused a deep sleep to fall upon the man
  and made Eve from Adam -- 2:21-22
Bone of my bones; flesh of my flesh ---2:23
Transparency: They were both naked,
  and were not ashamed ---2:25
Temptation: You shall not eat of every
  tree of the garden? --- 3:1
They realized they were naked; they were
  ashamed; they tried to cover themselves;
  and hid themselves -- 3:7-10
God will put enmity between the seed of the woman
  and the seed of the snake ---3:15
The Lord made clothes and covered them --3:21
The story of Nicodemus and being   **JOHN**
  born of the spirit ---3:1-8
And it was not Adam who was deceived,   **1 TIMOTHY**
  but the woman ---2:14

LESSON 2.1 Jesus Meets Our Personal Needs   **JOHN**
Jesus is the "Bread of Life"--- 6:49-54

LESSON 2.2 Our Union With Christ   **JOHN**
Believers are meaningful in ministry-- 14:12
Our union with Christ -- 14:20
Believers are Important   **2 CORINTHIANS**
  as ambassadors --- 5:17-21
                                                                                                EPHESIANS
Believers are totally accepted ---1:3-6
Believers are loved unconditionally --- 2:1-10
Believers are one with Christ as the
  head and the body are one --- 1:22-23
Believers are one with Christ as a
  building and its foundation are one --- 2:20-22

Alpha Series
Appendix

Believers are one with Christ as a
  husband and wife are one --- 5:31-32
PHILIPPIANS
Believers are adequate in power --- 4:13
COLOSSIANS
Believers are Forever forgiven --- 2:9-15

LESSON 3.1 Categories of Emotions
Man lives not by bread alone, but by **MATTHEW**
  every word from the mouth of God --- 4:4
Paul and Silas sing praises in the midst **ACTS**
  of their suffering in prison --- 16
ROMANS
For the wages of sin is death --- 6:23
EPHESIANS
Be angry but do not sin --- 4:26
Jesus can sympathize with us **HEBREWS**
  he was tempted like us --- 4:15

LESSON 3.2 Emotional Healing
ISAIAH
His suffering was predicted --- 53:3-6
Unless you change and become like children, **MATTHEW**
  you will never enter the kingdom of heaven --- 18:1-5
The wounded inward condition—
  To be healed: self-inflicted pain is needed. --- 18:7-10
The honesty of Jesus in the Garden --- 26:36-45
Jesus can sympathize with us **HEBREWS**
  he was tempted like us --- 4:15

LESSON 4.1 Traditions of Men
Create in me a clean heart, O God; **PSALM**
  and renew a right spirit within me --- 51:10
MATTHEW
Why don't Jesus' followers follow the law? --- 15:1-2
Teaching for doctrines the commandments of men --- 15:7-9
The dysfunction or defilement of sin does not
  come about by eating or drinking or drugging --- 15:11
The religious authorities were
  "blind leaders of the blind" --- 15:14
The things which defile the man come from the heart;

Alpha Series
Appendix

evil thoughts, murders, adulteries, i.e. (I will be worthy if...)	15:19-20
	EPHESIANS
Changing your thinking	4:17-24

LESSON 4.2 How Problems Develop.

If you continue in the word, you will know the truth,	**JOHN**
and the truth will make you free	8:31-32

LESSON 5.1 God's Regeneration Program

Human nature:	**ROMANS**
No one is good, nor righteous, not one	3:10-18
God's righteousness is a gift	3:21-28
We are now being saved from the habit, dominion and power of sin	Chps. 6-8
Do not be conformed to this world, but be transformed by the renewing of your mind	12:2
We have received, not the spirit of the world,	**1 CORINTHIANS**
but the Spirit who is from God	2:9-16
We are made right with God,	**GALATIANS**
not by law, but, by faith	2:16
It is no longer I who live, but, Christ who lives through me	2:20
Are you so foolish? Having begun by the Spirit, are you now being perfected by the flesh?	3:3
Walk by the Spirit, and you will not carry out the desire of the flesh	5:16
	EPHESIANS
Lay aside the old self; put on the new self, created in the likeness of God	4:17-23
For to me, to live is Christ,	**PHILIPPIANS**
and to die is gain	1:21
Have the attitude of humility just as Jesus did	2:5-9
	COLOSSIANS
Christ in you, the hope of glory	1:27
As you have received Christ, so walk in Him	2:6
You have died; your life is hidden with Christ	3:3

LESSON 5.2 The Promise of Victory

Consider yourselves	**ROMANS**

Alpha Series
Appendix

dead to sin and alive to God	6:11
Two lifestyles:	
faith (grace) and rejection (law)	6:12-14
Whatever is not of faith, is sin	14:23
In the past we were spiritually dead and should	**EPHESIANS**
have suffered Gods' anger	2:1-3

LESSON 6.1 The Old and New Covenants

DEUTERONOMY

The tithe ---------- 14:22-26

I will make a new agreement **JEREMIAH**
with the people of Israel
I will put my teachings in their minds
and write them on their hearts
all people will know me, from the least
to the most important,
I will not remember their sins anymore. ---------- 31:31-37

Completes the contrast between **2 CORINTHIANS**
law and grace in terms of glory ---------- Chapter 3

Our sufficiency is of God ---------- 3:5

LESSON 6.2 Slaves to Righteousness

Shall we sin, because we are not under **ROMANS**
the law, but under grace? God forbid! ---------- 6:15

An appeal to exercise responsibility in
realizing our new identity in Christ ---------- 6:19

Walk by the Spirit, and you will not **GALATIANS**
carry out the desire of the flesh.
If you are led by the Spirit,
you are not under the Law ---------- 5:16-18

The fruit of the Spirit ---------- 5:22-25

When we were dead in our **EPHESIANS**
transgressions, God made us alive.
By grace you have been saved through faith;
and that not of yourselves, it is the gift of God;
not as a result of works, that no one should boast.
For we are His workmanship, created in Christ Jesus
for good works, which God prepared beforehand,
that we should walk in them ---------- 2:4-10

LESSON 7.1 Dead to the Law

ROMANS

The law reveals sin ---------- 5:20
We have died with Christ, and have been freed from the law ---------- 6:6-10
A marriage analogy to illustrate the death of the law ---------- 7:1-4

Alpha Series
Appendix

The deadly interplay between the law and sin	7:7-13
The sting of death is sin,	**1 CORINTHIANS**
and the power of sin is the law.	15:56
The promise is given *through faith*	**GALATIANS**
to people who believe in Jesus Christ	3:22-23
Circumcised with a spiritual circumcision,	**COLOSSIANS**

Buried with him in baptism, raised with him
  through faith in the power of God,
God has erased the record against us,
  nailing it to the cross ---------- 2:10-14

LESSON 7.2 Conflict Without Condemnation   ROMANS
Consider yourselves dead to sin, and alive to God in Christ Jesus ------------ 6:11
The law is spiritual: but I am carnal;
  I do not do what I want,
  but I do the very thing I hate ---------- 7:14-15
O wretched man that I am!
  Who shall deliver me from
  the body of this death? ---------- 7:24

New Testament do's and don'ts (more law):
Love others as Christ loves them	**JOHN**	13:34-35
Pray without ceasing	**1 THESSALONIANS**	5:17
Do not be weary in well doing	**GALATIANS**	6:9
Think of others more than ourselves	**PHILIPPIANS**	2:2-4
Never worry	**PHILIPPIANS**	4:6

LESSON 8.1 The Freedom of the Spirit   JOHN
What is born of the Spirit is up to the Spirit ---------- 3:5-8
Jesus speaks of the Holy Spirit Who
  is to be given to all believers ---------- 7:37-39
The Spirit abides in us and is with us ---------- 14:17
                                                    ROMANS
Life after the flesh ---------- 1:18-32
Life after the flesh ---------- 3:10-18
The righteous life of Christ imputed is
  to all who believe on Him ---------- 3:21-24; 5:1-12
We are buried with Christ in baptism,
  raised with him to newness of life ---------- 6:4
We have been freed from sin, and
  became slaves of righteousness ---------- 6:18
We are released from the law
  to serve in newness of the Spirit ---------- 7:4-6

Alpha Series
Appendix

Wretched man that I am who will set me free?	7:23-24
The requirement of the law is fulfilled in us who walk not by the flesh, but by the Spirit	8:3-4

1 CORINTHIANS

We have the Spirit who is from God, that we might know the things freely given to us by God	2:9-14
Your body is a temple of the Holy Spirit who is in you	6:19
For by one Spirit we were all baptized into one body	12:13

2 CORINTHIANS

God made Jesus to be sin so we might become the righteousness of God	5:21

GALATIANS

The works of the flesh	5:19-21
The works of the Spirit	5:22-23

EPHESIANS

Having believed in him, we were marked with the seal of the promised Holy Spirit; this is the guarantee of our inheritance	1:13-14
We were once dead in our sins, by nature children of wrath	2:1-3
Do not live based upon the futility of your own thinking	4:17-19
Do not grieve the Holy Spirit with whom you have been marked	4:30;

PHILIPPIANS

As you therefore have received Christ Jesus the Lord, continue to live your lives in him, rooted and built up in him and established in the faith	2:5-8

LESSON 8.2 The Call To Faith

In order to see the kingdom of God	**JOHN**
you must be born again	3:3
We live by the Spirit of God within us	**ROMANS**
instead of the pre-conditioning of our flesh	8:9-13
What you do or do not do does not	**GALATIANS**
count with God all that counts is faith	5:5-6
Live by the Spirit, not by the flesh	5:16-17
Get rid of the deeds of the flesh since	**COLOSSIANS**
you have been clothed with your new self	3:5-10

LESSON 9.1 Personal Assurance of the Spirit

My sheep hear my voice,	**JOHN**
and I know them	10:27
Jesus promises the Holy spirit who will live in us	14:16-18
We are children of God and have	**ROMANS**

Alpha Series
Appendix

received the spirit of adoption instead of the spirit of slavery leading to fear	8:14-17
You are no longer a slave but a child, and also an heir, through God	4:6-7
Be not drunk with wine;	**EPHESIANS**
but be filled with the Spirit	5:18
Grieving the Spirit	4:30
	1 THESSALONIANS
Quenching the Spirit	5:19
The Word of God is a two edged sword;	**HEBREWS**
able to judge the thoughts of the heart	4:12

LESSON 9.2 Facing Trials in the Spirit

The benefits of being justified by faith in Jesus	**ROMANS**
through peace and tribulations	5:1-5
Being children of God and joint heirs with Christ involves suffering as well as glory	8:17
The eternal view of suffering: The sufferings we have now are nothing compared to the great glory that will be shown to us	8:18-23
The Hope: Everything will be set free from ruin to have God's freedom	8:19-21
From the eternal view of God, we were predestined, called, justified, and glorified before the world was created	8:30
Who or what can be against us if God is for us? Who can accuse us before God? Who can condemn us? (Shall Christ condemn us?) Who or what can separate us from God's love?	8:31-39
Small troubles now, help us gain an	**2 CORINTHIANS**
eternal glory much greater than the troubles. We set our eyes not on what we see but on what we cannot see. What we see will last only a short time, but what we cannot see will last forever	4:17-18

THE ETERNAL VIEW:

DO NOT BE SURPRISED	1 Peter 4:12-14
Because of union with Christ	John 15:18
For the sake of Christ	Philippians 1:27
As a testimony to others	1 Peter 3:13
SEE THE END AT THE BEGINNING	2 Corinthainas 4:17-18
God's love	Romans 5:3-5
Joy unspeakable	1 Peter 1:3-9

Alpha Series
Appendix

Peaceable fruit of righteousness	Hebrews 12:1-11
Spiritual maturity	James 1:2-4
KNOW YOU CANNOT LOSE	1 John 5:4
With trial comes grace	2 Corinthians 10:13
God is in absolute control	1 Corinthians 10:13
All things work for good	Romans 8:28
More than conquerors	Romans 8:37

LESSON 10.1 Relational Ministry

God proved His love while we were yet sinners	**ROMANS**
Jesus died for us	5:8
For God so loved the world	**JOHN**
that He gave His only Son	3:16
Jesus loves his disciples as a servant	13:1-17
	1 JOHN
Love others as God loves us	4:7-11
God is love	4:16
Jesus Christ is the same yesterday	**HEBREWS**
and today, yes and forever	13:8
	JAMES
All good things come from God	1:17

LESSON 10.2 Comfort In Relational Ministry

	JOHN
I am the way, the truth, and the life:	4:6
The Central command for relational ministry: love one another	13:34-35
Greater works than these shall he do	14:12
Ask for anything in my name,...so the Father's glory will be shown through the Son	14:13

LESSON 11.1 The Vine and the Branches

The Son can do nothing alone. The Son does whatever the Father does.	**JOHN** 5:19
These things I do are not by my own authority but that I say only what the Father has taught me	8:28-29
The Father and I are one	10:30
I am the one God chose and sent into the world	10:36
Then you will know and understand that the Father is in me and I am in the Father	10:38
Whoever has seen me has seen the Father	14:9
The Father lives in me and does his own work	14:10
I am in the Father and the Father is in me	14:11

Alpha Study Guide Bibile References

Alpha Series
Appendix

Because I live, ye shall live also. At that day ye shall know that I am in my Father, and ye in me, and I in you	14:19-20
I am the true vine; my Father is the vine grower YOU ARE THE BRANCHES	15:1-8
Father, I pray that they can be one. As you are in me and I am in you, I pray that they can also be one in us	17:21-22
If we walk in the light, we have fellowship with one another, and the blood of Jesus His Son cleanses us from all sin	**1 JOHN** 1:7
For anyone who lacks these things is nearsighted and blind, and is forgetful of the cleansing of past sins	**2 PETER** 1:9

LESSON 11.2 Living In Christ's Love

God loved the world so much that he gave his one and only Son so that whoever believes in him may not be lost, but have eternal life.	**JOHN** 3:16
As the *Father* hath loved me, so have I loved you: keep my commandments; abide in my love; as I have kept my Father's commandments, and abide in His love	15:9-10
I have told you these things so that you can have the same joy I have and so that your joy will be the fullest possible joy	15:11
Love each other as I have loved you	12-13
Let us look only to Jesus, the One who began our faith and who makes it perfect. He suffered death on the cross. But he accepted the shame as if it were nothing because of the joy that God put before him. And now he is sitting at the right side of God's throne	**HEBREWS** 12:2
But you believe in him. So you are filled with a joy that cannot be explained, a joy full of glory	**1 PETER** 1:8

LESSON 12.1 The Ministry of the Overcomer

Welcome those who are weak in faith, but not for the purpose of quarreling over opinions	**ROMANS** 14:1
God comforts us in all our tribulation, that we may be able to comfort others that are in any trouble	**2 CORINTHIANS** 1:3-4
Examine yourselves to see whether you are living in the faith. Test yourselves. Do you not realize that Jesus Christ is in you?	

Alpha Series
Appendix

Unless, indeed, you fail to meet the test!	13:5
True leadership:	**EPHESIANS**
Equipping of the saints	4:11-16
Admonish the unruly, encourage	**1 THESSALONIANS**
the fainthearted, help the weak,	
be patient with all men	5:14
For whatsoever is born of God overcometh	**1 JOHN**
the world, even our faith. Who is he that	
overcometh the world, but he that believeth	
that Jesus is the Son of God?	5:4-5
Brethren, if a man be overtaken in a	**GALATIANS**
fault, ye which are spiritual, restore such	
a one in the spirit of meekness; considering	
thyself, lest thou also be tempted	6:1

LESSON 12.2 The Overcomer's Church

The first mention of the church:	**MATTHEW**
upon this Rock I will build My church	
and the gates of Hades shall not prevail	
against it. I will give you the keys to the	
kingdom	16:13-19
The ministry of reconciliation:	**2 CORINTHIANS**
God has made us to be new creations;	
He has reconciled himself to us	
He has made us to be ambassadors	
be reconciled to him	5:17-6:2
The basis of the church:	**1 PETER**
Come to the Lord Jesus, the "stone"	
that lives. You also are like living stones,	
his stone is worth much to you who believe	
But to the people who do not believe, "the	
stone that the builders rejected has become the	
cornerstone." But you are a chosen people,	
royal priests, a holy nation, a people for God's own	
possession. You were chosen to tell about	
the wonderful acts of God, who called	
you out of darkness into his wonderful light.	
Dear friends, you are like foreigners and strangers	
in this world. People who do not believe are	
living all around you and might say that you	
are doing wrong	2:4-12